TOP 10 MARRAKECH

ANDREW HUMPHREYS

EYEWITNESS TRAVEL

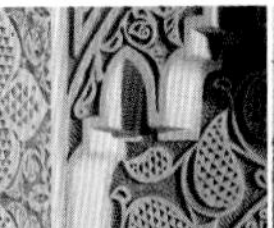

Left **Souks** Centre **Saadian Tombs** Right **City walls**

LONDON, NEW YORK,
MELBOURNE, MUNICH AND DELHI
www.dk.com

Design, Editorial, and Picture Research, by Quadrum Solutions, Krishnamai, 33B, Sir Pochkanwala Road, Worli, Mumbai, India.

Printed and bound in China by Leo Paper Products Ltd.

First American Edition, 2008

14 15 16 17 10 9 8 7 6 5 4 3 2 1

Published in the United States by DK Publishing, 345 Hudson Street, New York, New York 10014

Reprinted with revisions 2010, 2012, 2014

Published in Great Britain by Dorling Kindersley Limited

A catalog record for this book is available from the Library of Congress
ISSN 1479-344X
ISBN 978-1-46541-038-2

Within each Top 10 list in this book, no hierarchy of quality or popularity is implied. All 10 are, in the editor's opinion, of roughly equal merit.

Floors are referred to throughout in accordance with British usage; ie the "first floor" is the floor above ground level.

MIX
Paper from responsible sources
FSC™ C018179

Contents

Marrakech's Top 10

Marrakech Highlights 6

Jemaa El Fna 8

The Night Market 10

Koutoubia Mosque 12

The Souks 14

City Walls and Gates 18

Saadian Tombs 20

Medersa Ben Youssef 22

Badii Palace 24

Majorelle Gardens 26

Mamounia Hotel 28

Moments in History 32

Celebrity Visitors 34

The information in this DK Eyewitness Top 10 Travel Guide is checked regularly.

Every effort has been made to ensure that this book is as up-to-date as possible at the time of going to press. Some details, however, such as telephone numbers, opening hours, prices, gallery hanging arrangements and travel information are liable to change. The publishers cannot accept responsibility for any consequences arising from the use of this book, nor for any material on third party websites, and cannot guarantee that any website address in this book will be a suitable source of travel information. We value the views and suggestions of our readers very highly. Please write to: Publisher, DK Eyewitness Travel Guides, Dorling Kindersley, 80 Strand, London WC2R 0RL, or email: travelguides@dk.com.

Cover: Front – **Corbis:** Calle Montes/Photononstop main; **DK Images:** Alan Keohane clb. Spine – **DK Images:** Alan Keohane b. Back – **DK Images:** Alan Keohane tl,tc,tr.

Left **Camel trekking** Centre **Galerie Damgaard, Essaouira** Right **Atlas Mountains**

Moroccan Architecture 36

Modern Moroccan Styles 38

Hammams and Spas 40

Parks and Gardens 42

Arts and Culture 44

Riads 46

Marrakech for Children 48

Moroccan Cuisine 50

Restaurants 52

Nightlife 54

Day Trips 56

Around Town

Jemaa El Fna and the Kasbah 60

The Souks 66

The New City 74

Essaouira 80

Tizi-n-Test Pass 88

Tizi-n-Tichka Pass 94

Streetsmart

Practical Information 102

Places to Stay 111

General Index 118

Phrase Book 126

Left **Kasbah Mosque** Right **Spa jacuzzi at La Sultana**

Key to abbreviations **Adm** *admission charge* **Credit cards** *MC = MasterCard, V = Visa, AmEx = American Express*

MARRAKECH'S TOP 10

Marrakech Highlights 6–7

Jemaa El Fna 8–9

The Night Market 10–11

Koutoubia Mosque 12–13

The Souks 14–17

City Walls and Gates 18–19

Saadian Tombs 20–21

Medersa Ben Youssef 22–23

Badii Palace 24–25

Majorelle Gardens 26–27

Mamounia Hotel 28–29

Top Ten of Everything 32–57

TOP 10 Marrakech Highlights

An oasis in every sense of the word, Marrakech was once a beacon for the trading caravans that had driven north through the desert and navigated over the often snow-capped Atlas Mountains. Marrakech may be Morocco's third most important city after Rabat and Casablanca, but its fabulous palaces and palm groves exercise a powerful hold over tourists. It has always been the place where sub-Saharan Africa meets Arab North Africa, and, even today, this market town located on the edge of nowhere remains a compellingly exotic port of call.

1 Jemaa El Fna

This is a vast plaza at the heart of the medina (the old walled city), as old as Marrakech itself. The site of parades and executions in the past, modern city life is centred around the Jemaa El Fna *(see pp8–9)*.

2 The Night Market

By night, Jemaa El Fna transforms into a circus, theatre and restaurant, with itinerant musicians and entertainers drawing excitable crowds *(see pp10–11)*.

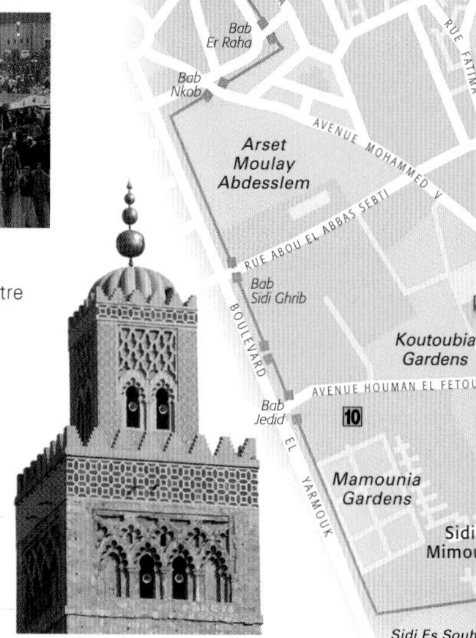

3 Koutoubia Mosque

Marrakech's landmark monument boasts a tower that dominates the skyline for miles around. Like most mosques in Morocco, it is closed to non-Muslims but it's an impressive sight nonetheless *(see pp12–13)*.

4 The Souks

Laid out in the narrow streets to the north of central Jemaa El Fna are a dizzying array of souks, or bazaars. Different areas specialize in their own specific wares, selling anything from carpets, lanterns and slippers, to ingredients for magic spells *(see pp14–15)*.

Preceding pages **City Walls along Agdal Gardens**

5 City Walls and Gates

Marrakech's medina, or old city, is wrapped around by several miles of reddish-pink, dried mud walls, punctuated by nearly 20 gates. Having proved ineffective against attackers throughout history, the walls are more ornamental than functional *(see pp18–19)*.

Saadian Tombs 6

A tranquil garden hidden at the end of the narrowest of meandering passageways shelters the royal tombs of one of Morocco's ruling dynasties. They were shrouded from the world till the 1920s *(see pp20–21)*.

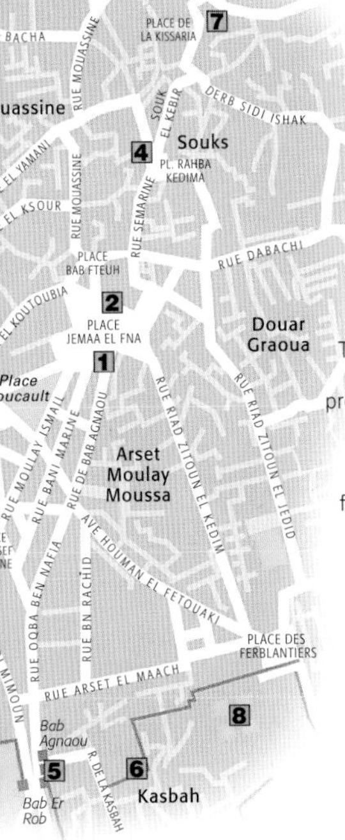

7 Medersa Ben Youssef

Behind a typically blank Marrakech façade hides what is arguably the city's finest building. This ancient religious school boasts exquisite decorative detail *(see pp22–3)*.

Badii Palace 8

The ruins of this once fabled palace provide a picturesque setting for nesting storks – and a salutary warning from history against extravagance *(see pp24–5)*.

9 Majorelle Gardens

Jacques Majorelle, a French artist who came to Marrakech to recuperate, created this beautiful garden which was later owned by French couturier, Yves Saint-Laurent. It is open to the public *(see pp26–7)*.

10 Mamounia Hotel

A *grande dame* among hotels worldwide, the Mamounia has been providing hospitality to the visiting rich and famous for almost a century *(see pp28–9)*.

Top 10 Jemaa El Fna

The medina's central square means "Assembly of the Dead", a reference to a time when the heads of executed criminals would be displayed here on spikes. Although nothing as gruesome is on view today, the square is still populated with some extraordinary sights such as snake charmers, acrobats and colourfully costumed water sellers. In spite of government efforts to sanitize Jemaa El Fna with neat paving and ornamental barrows, the place remains endearingly chaotic.

1 Orange-Juice Stalls

The first to appear on the square every morning are these sellers of freshly squeezed orange juice. They work in brightly painted iron barrows fringing the square.

Dried fruit and nuts stall

It is worth paying repeated visits at different times of the day, but in summer months the square goes uncharacteristically quiet during the hottest part of the afternoon.

Chez Chegrouni and the Terrasses de l'Alhambra are good lunch spots *(see p65)* and both offer upper terrace seating overlooking the square.

- *Map J3*
- *Medina*
- *Café de France: 0524 44 32 19; open 6am–11pm daily; closes late in summer; two restaurants; no credit cards accepted*
- *Calèche rides: Place Foucault, off Jemaa El Fna; prices are listed for specific tours, or negotiate an hourly rate of about 90 Dh*

Top 10 Features

1. Orange-Juice Stalls
2. Snake Charmers
3. Café de France
4. Calèches
5. Water Sellers
6. Porters
7. Tooth Pullers
8. Acrobats
9. Herbalists
10. Fortune Tellers

2 Snake Charmers

The heat makes the snakes unresponsive so the charmers work on tourists, cajoling them into draping the lethargic reptiles over their shoulders for a photograph.

3 Café de France

There are several places to sit and watch the incessant entertainment of the square over coffee but the raffish air of the Café de France *(left)* lends it an added appeal and is a favourite with tourists and locals alike.

For Jemaa El Fna by night, **see pp10–11.**

4 Calèches

Hop into one of the waiting *calèches*, or horse-drawn carriages *(above)*, parked along the square's west side. For a fee – you may need to bargain down from the driver's inflated price – you can take a circuit of the city walls, or almost anywhere you care to go.

5 Water Sellers

Known by the locals as *gerrab*, the water sellers roam the square in colourful costumes and tassel-fringed hats, ringing copper bells to announce their arrival *(centre)*. The brass cups are meant exclusively for the Muslims, while the white-metal cups are for the thirsty people from all other religions.

6 Porters

With cars banned from crossing Jemaa El Fna, access to many of the hotels in the surrounding alleys is provided by the ubiquitous porter *(carroser)*, who carries your luggage on a wheeled barrow and transports it to your lodgings for a small tip.

7 Tooth Pullers

These self-proclaimed "dentists" sit behind wooden trays filled with loose teeth ready to aid cash-poor locals with aching dentures.

8 Acrobats

An array of acrobats and athletic young men *(above)* perform spectacular feats to entertain the audience and earn a few coins. Their repertoire usually includes cartwheels, somersaults and tottering pyramids.

9 Herbalists

These *(above)* stand as testimony to the Moroccan belief in natural remedies. Compounds of ground roots, dried herbs and even desiccated animal parts are used for everything, from curing head colds to warding off the evil eye.

10 Fortune Tellers

Throughout the day, impossibly wrinkled, elderly women squat beneath umbrellas with packs of Tarot cards to hold forth on the fortunes of the people who drop by for a reading.

An Unplanned Masterpiece

Jemaa El Fna is considered to be a "Masterpiece of the Oral and Intangible Heritage of Humanity", according to the UNESCO. This is an international list that includes pieces of intangible culture such as song cycles, theatrical traditions and sacred spaces. Inclusion in the list is intended to raise awareness and preserve something unique and irreplaceable; Jemaa El Fna certainly qualifies.

For dining and shopping options in this area, **see pp64–5.**

TOP 10 The Night Market

Each evening as the sun goes down, dozens of open-air kitchens set up on the east side of Jemaa El Fna. Serving areas are erected and tables and benches are put out to create one vast alfresco eatery. Beneath a hanging cloud of smoke from the crackling charcoal grills, locals and visitors alike tuck into a vast array of Moroccan cuisine. Nearly every stall has its own speciality, from snails in spicy broth and chunks of lamb stuffed into sandwiches to humble hard-boiled eggs.

A dry-fruit stall

Although Marrakech has a very low crime rate, the crowds milling around Jemaa El Fna at night are perfect cover for pickpockets. Be careful with handbags and wallets.

If you find the food stalls at the Night Market to be intimidating, you can always opt for the relative familiarity of salads, pizza and pasta at the Terrasses de l'Alhambra *(see p65)* instead.

- *Map J3*
- *The Night Market sets up at sunset daily and runs until around midnight, or later in the summer months.*
- *Café Glacier: 0524 44 21 93; Open 6am–10:30pm daily*

Top 10 Features

1. The food
2. Hygiene
3. Etiquette
4. Entertainers
5. Storytellers
6. Transvestite dancers
7. Musicians
8. Majoun
9. Café Glacier
10. Henna painting

1 The food

Some of the most popular eatables are the varieties of *brochette* – grilled lamb and chicken – along with bowls of soup, spicy sausages, grilled fish and bowls of boiled chickpeas.

2 Hygiene

The raw ingredients arrive fresh each evening and the food is cooked in front of you. Plates and utensils are often washed in water that isn't changed for much of the night, so get your food served on paper and eat with your fingers.

3 Etiquette

Walk around to view what's on offer and when you see something you like, take a seat. You don't have to speak Arabic – just point to what you want. Prices are usually posted and everything is inexpensive.

4 Entertainers

Knots of excited onlookers surround a menagerie of tricksters, sundry wild-eyed performers and fortune tellers *(below)*. This is where the Moroccan belief in everyday magic is on full display. And it's not put on for tourists.

For more information on Moroccan cuisine, **see pp50–51.**

5 Storytellers

Gifted orators enthral their rapt audience with tales of Islamic heroes and buffoons. Sessions end on a cliffhanger – the outcome is revealed only on the following night.

6 Transvestite dancers

You'll find men who dance wildly while dressed in women's clothing *(right)*. It's an age-old practice – one that lends a slightly surreal, almost cultic air, to the goings-on on the square.

7 Musicians

A smattering of musicians and, often, groups of Gnawa *(below)*, who specialize in hypnotic, thrumming rhythms, entrance crowds of listeners who stand around swaying in far-off reveries, long after everyone else has called it a night.

8 Majoun

The wild-eyed appearance of some of the denizens of Jemaa El Fna is caused by the consumption of this hallucinogenic, marijuana-based drug. Sold as jam-like tablets, it is best avoided.

9 Café Glacier

One of the best places from which to observe the spectacle of the Jemaa El Fna at night is from the rooftop terrace of Café Glacier, located at the southern edge. The best time to visit is as the sun sets.

10 Henna painting

Day or night, ladies with piping bags full of henna paste paint hands and feet with the most intricate of designs *(above)*. Be aware that sometimes an illegal colouring substance that can cause severe skin problems is used – approach with caution.

The Gnawa

The Gnawa came to Morocco as slaves from sub-Saharan Africa. Over the centuries they have kept alive their culture through oral traditions and, particularly, music. Played on simple string instruments known as *gimbri*, their music is looping and repetitive, intended to produce an almost trance-like state in the dancers and vocalists who sometimes accompany the musicians. Gnawa music has made a great impact on the global world music scene.

During the International Film Festival a large screen is erected on Jemaa El Fna, **see p44.**

Top 10 Koutoubia Mosque

Its minaret is the city's pre-eminent monument, towering above all else and has always been the first visible sign of Marrakech for travellers approaching from afar. This is wholly fitting, because the mosque is not only the city's main place of worship, it is also one of the city's oldest buildings, dating back to the 12th century, not long after Marrakech was founded. The designer of the Koutoubia minaret went on to create Tour Hassan in the Moroccan capital, Rabat and the tower of the Giralda in Seville. Unfortunately, as with nearly all mosques and shrines in Morocco, non-Muslims are not permitted to enter the Koutoubia.

The Prayer Hall entrance

Although access is denied to non-Muslims, one of the doors on the east wall is often open and you can peer through for a view of the impressive main prayer hall and its seemingly endless arcades of horseshoe arches.

Pizzeria Venezia ***(see p65)*****, which is just across the road from the Koutoubia, has a rooftop terrace that offers excellent views of the mosque and minaret.**

- *Map H4*
- *Avenue Bab Jedid, Medina*
- *Mosque: Open only during prayer times (see right); closed to all non-Muslims*
- *Gardens: free entry to both Muslims and non-Muslims*

Top 10 Features

1. Mosque of the Booksellers
2. Minaret
3. The minaret decoration
4. The mosque plan
5. Prayer times
6. Ruins of the Almohad Mosque
7. Dar El Hajar
8. Koubba Lalla Zohra
9. Koutoubia Gardens
10. Tomb of Yousef Ben Tachfine

1 Mosque of the Booksellers

The Koutoubia was built in 1158. Its name means the Mosque of the Booksellers, which is a reference to a small market that once existed in the neighbourhood, where worshippers could buy copies of religious tracts.

2 Minaret

The purpose of a minaret is to provide a high platform from which the *muezzin* can make the five-times-daily call to prayer. Rather than a staircase, the Koutoubia's towering minaret *(left)* has a spiralling ramp wide enough for a horse to be ridden to the top.

For more information on Islam and the regulations for visiting mosques, **see p106.**

3 The minaret decoration

Originally the whole minaret was encased in tiles and carved stucco, but now only two shallow bands of blue ceramics remain.

4 The mosque plan

The mosque is rectangular in plan. The relatively plain main east entrance leads to a vast prayer hall with its eight bays and horseshoe arches. North of the prayer hall is a courtyard with fountains and trees.

5 Prayer times

Exact times of daily prayer change with the seasons, but are observed pre-dawn, noon, late afternoon, sunset and late evening, as indicated by the *muezzin*. The most important prayers of the week are those at noon on Friday.

6 Ruins of the Almohad Mosque

Next to the Koutoubia are the remains of an earlier mosque, circa 1147. The bases of the prayer hall's columns, secured behind railings, are clearly visible *(left)*. They were revealed during excavations by Moroccan archaeologists.

7 Dar El Hajar

Two wells on the piazza allow visitors to view the buried remains of the Dar El Hajar, a fortress built by the Almoravids. It was destroyed when the Almohads captured the city *(see p32)*.

8 Koubba Lalla Zohra

This white tomb *(below)* houses the body of Lalla Zohra – a slave's daughter who transformed into a dove each night.

9 Koutoubia Gardens

South of the mosque is a garden with a mix of palms and deciduous trees, topiary hedges and colourful roses *(centre)*.

10 Tomb of Yousef Ben Tachfine

Just north of the mosque, glimpsed through a locked gate, is a walled area containing the dilapidated mausoleum of Yousef Ben Tachfine, tribal leader of the Almoravids, and the man credited with the founding of Marrakech.

Heights of Good Taste

The Koutoubia minaret's continued domination of the skyline is owed largely to an enlightened piece of legislation by the city's former French colonial rulers. It was they who decreed that no building in the medina should rise above the height of a palm tree, and that no building in the New City should rise above the height of the Koutoubia's minaret. The ruling holds good even today. Only Muslims may enjoy the great view from the top of the building.

For more information on the elements of Moroccan architecture, **see pp36–7.**

TOP 10 The Souks

Marrakech's earliest inhabitants made their living from trading with the Africans and with the Spaniards who came by sea. Luxuries like gold and ivory came from the south, while leather, metalwork and ceramics were sent north. Even today, trade continues to be the city's mainstay, with thousands of craftsmen eking out an existence in the maze of souks that fill much of the northern half of the medina. A trip to the souks is part history lesson, part endurance test – to see how long you can keep your purse in your bag or your wallet in your pocket.

Metalwork on display

You will get lost in the souks. Alleys are narrow, winding and constantly branching, while landmarks are few. However, the area covered is small and you are never more than a few minutes' walk back to Jemaa El Fna. Locals are friendly and will point out the way.

Café Arabe, near the Souk des Teinturiers, and Café des Epices in the Rahba Kedima are both great places to relax with a mint tea and a light snack *(see p71)*.

- *Map K2*
- *Medina*
- *Many shops in the souks are closed on Friday*

Top 10 Features

1. Rue Semarine
2. Souk El Kebir
3. Souk des Babouches
4. Souk des Tapis
5. Souk des Teinturiers
6. Souk des Ferronniers
7. Fondouks
8. Souk El Khemis
9. Souk El Bab Salaam
10. Rahba Kedima

1 Rue Semarine

The main route into the souks is via an arch just north of Jemaa El Fna and along this perpetually busy, sun-dappled alley. Shop owners along Semarine attempt to entice with a miscellany of robes, kaftans, carpets and antiques.

2 Souk El Kebir

Straight on from Rue Semarine, this is the heart of the souks. It's a narrow alley that lurches from side-to-side and up-and-down. It is lined by dozens of the tiniest shops – barely a person wide – each overflowing with goods, particularly leather.

3 Souk des Babouches

Every shop and stall here sells nothing but brightly-coloured, soft-leather, pointy-toed slippers known as *babouches*.

For more places to shop in and around the souks, **see p70.**

4 Souk des Tapis

Earlier an auction place for slaves, this souk is now crowded with a number of carpet sellers *(left)*.

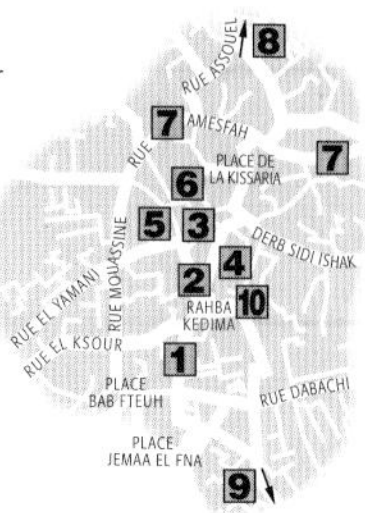

5 Souk des Teinturiers

Sheaves of freshly dyed wool *(below)* are hung from ropes strung across one particular alleyway for a vibrantly colourful scene.

6 Souk des Ferronniers

Multiple hammering sounds fill the air in the medina's medieval parts where the ironworkers *(below)* create furniture, lanterns and other items.

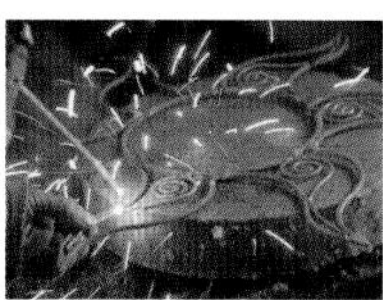

7 Fondouks

The fondouk is an ancient hostelry for travelling merchants built around a courtyard. Most are now gritty workshops.

8 Souk El Khemis

Entrepreneurs renovating riads scout this flea market to the north of the medina for unusual items of furniture.

9 Souk El Bab Salaam

This covered market serves the nearby mellah quarter with everything from food and spices to caged birds.

10 Rahba Kedima

This open square is home to sellers of dried scorpions, leeches and other bizarre substances and objects for use in *sihacen*, or black magic.

The guide issue

A guide to the souks is really not necessary. Although the souks are a warren, the area is not too large and it's never hard to find your way back to some familiar landmark. Any "best places" your guide may lead you to are only best by virtue of offering your guide the highest of commissions.

For more on fondouks, **see p67.**

Left **Akkal ceramic** Right **Babouches**

Top 10 Marrakech Souvenirs

1 Babouches

Babouches are Moroccan slippers, handmade from local leather, although increasingly the babouches found in the souks are made of a synthetic plastic that only looks like leather. In their most basic form they are pointy-toed and come in a variety of colours – canary yellow being the most common – but are otherwise plain. Increasingly however, boutiques and shops are customizing their babouches with silk trim, or even carving the leather with exquisite designs.

2 Argan oil

Argan oil is an almost mystical substance to which all kinds of properties are attributed *(see p90)*. Part of its mystique can be credited to the rarity of argan trees, which only grow in southwestern Morocco. The oil is sold all over the souks but much of it is low grade. For quality oil, it's best to buy from a reputable dealer.

Fruit of the argan tree

Fanous lantern

3 Carpets

Marrakech is famed for its carpets, made by the tribes of the south. Each tribe has its own patterns. Beware the salesmen's patter. Some carpets are very old and made of genuine cactus silk but these are rare. Most sold today, though beautiful, are quite modern and made from non-natural fibres. Buy a carpet if you like it, and not because you have been told that it's a good investment.

4 Pottery

Each region of Morocco produces its own distinctive pottery. The local style is plain terracotta finished with colourful glazes. Ceramics from the Akkal factory would not look out of place in a cutting edge design shop. Or visit the big pottery souk outside Bab Ghemat which is to the south-east of the medina.

5 Lanterns

There are two types of lanterns: those that hang from the ceiling and those that sit on the floor. The former (known as *fanous*) are typically fashioned from metal and come in elaborate shapes with intricate decoration. The latter are made of skin and goats' hair and are usually colourful. Look for them in the northern part of the souk or down at the Place des Ferblantiers.

6 Leather bags

Marrakech is known for its leather. It is made by treating animal hides by hand in the tanneries *(see p68)* in the east of the medina which are then dyed. Unsurprisingly, the shops of the souk are filled with leather goods from purses to handbags to book bindings. Do plenty of window shopping before settling on an item.

Leather bag

7 Candles

Candles are used to great effect in local restaurants. They are sold in all shapes, colours and sizes in the souk, and some of the designs can be highly inventive. Some of the best are made by a small company called Amira *(www.amirabougies.com)* and you can buy them in various boutiques.

8 Jewellery

The local Berber jewellery is silver, chunky and heavy. However, a number of artisans in Marrakech, both local and foreign, produce more modern designs. Look out for Joanna Bristow's brilliant designs in select hotel boutiques such as Amanjena *(see p117)*.

Jewellery

9 Fashion

Marrakech has inspired countless foreign couturiers – from Yves Saint-Laurent to Tom Ford. However, the city now has a fashion of its own. There are some young Moroccan designers producing beautiful clothing, like the high-profile brothers behind the boutique Beldi, first established in the 1940s, whose collections made from local fabric are tailored to Western sensibilities *(see p70)*.

10 Marra-Kitsch

A trend among local designers involves taking the iconography of Marrakech and giving it a Pop-ish twist. Chic store Atelier Moro designs its own distinctive clothing and sells original jewellery by local designers. Hassan Hajjaj makes *fanous* from sheets of tin printed with advertising logos, sold at his Riad Yima, approximately five minutes from Jemaa El Fna *(www.riadyima.com)*.

Pile of carpets in the Souk des Tapis

City Walls and Gates

The city walls date from the 1120s when, under threat of attack from the Almohads of the south, the ruling Almoravid sultan, Ali Ben Youssef, decided to encircle his garrison town with fortifications. The walls he had built were up to 9 m (30 ft) high and formed a circuit of 10 km (6 miles), punctuated by some 200 towers and 20 gates. Despite changes made in the 20th century to accommodate motor vehicles, the walls remain largely unchanged.

Top 10 Features

1. Pisé
2. Bab Agnaou
3. Bab El Rob
4. Bab Doukkala
5. Bab Berrima
6. Bab Debbagh
7. Bab El Khemis
8. The Seven Saints
9. Dar El Haoura
10. *Calèche* tours

Bab Doukkala

Walking a circuit around the outside of the walls is tiring and can be unpleasant as they are edged by major roads. Better to visit the gates individually or take a *calèche* tour.

If you take a *calèche* ride around the walls, make sure that you carry bottled water, as it can get hot and dusty.

- *Medina*
- *Bab Debbagh: permission required to access the roof (not always open to visitors)*
- Calèche *rides: Place Foucault, off Jemaa El Fna; Prices are listed for specific tours, or negotiate an hourly rate of about 90 Dh*

1 Pisé

The walls are built from a mixture of mud, straw and lime (known as pisé), which becomes as hard as brick on drying. The distinctive pinkish-red hue of the walls *(below)* is a result of pigments in the local earth.

2 Bab Agnaou

The most beautiful city gate, the "Gate of the Gnawa", is the only stone-built one *(right)*. It was erected during Almohad sultan Yacoub El Mansour's reign.

3 Bab El Rob

This was the original southern city gate *(right)*. The gatehouse building is now occupied by a pottery shop and all foot and car traffic pass through a modern breach in the old walls.

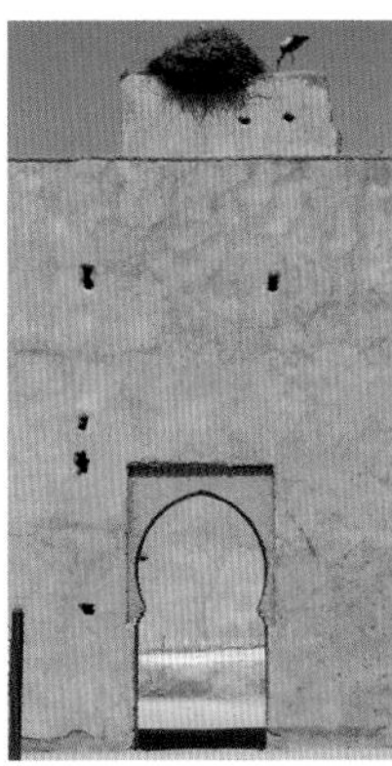

4 Bab Doukkala

This massive gate *(top left)* built by the Almoravids in the 12th century now stands isolated from the walls, thanks to 20th-century urban planning. The cavernous interior rooms lend themselves for use as a sometime event space.

5 Bab Berrima

Apart from being perimeter defences, other walls and gates divided up the interior of the medina. For instance, a wall separated the royal kasbah quarter from the city; Bab Berrima was one of the gates between these two distinct zones.

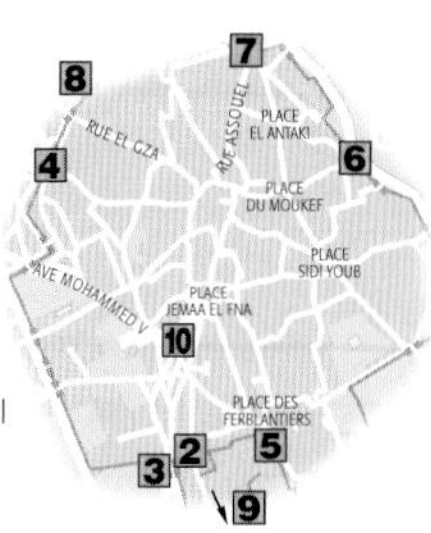

6 Bab Debbagh

This gate gives access to the tanneries, and when it's open to visitors you can ascend an internal staircase to the gatehouse roof for sweeping city views.

7 Bab El Khemis

The most northerly of gates *(above)* is also the most decorative, with a semi-circle of stalactite mouldings arcing over the entranceway. Outside the gate is a pretty little *marabout* or shrine.

8 The Seven Saints

Just outside the walls stand seven stone towers, each topped by a tree. This giant ensemble is in homage to the seven saints of Marrakech *(see p68)*.

9 Dar El Haoura

West of the Agdal Gardens, this curious free-standing fortress used to be a garrison for cavalry and its horse ramp is intact to this day.

10 Calèche tours

The best way to view the walls is by a *calèche* *(see pp8–9)*. You can take a complete circuit for the equivalent of a few pounds.

The Red City

Marrakech's distinctive colouring is from pigments in the local soil, mixed to make *pisé* from which its buildings have traditionally been constructed. In the last century, this was threatened by new building materials such as concrete. Therefore the ruling French decreed that all new buildings be painted pink. This rule continues to be in force even today, with pleasing results.

Saadian Tombs

This is the secluded burial place of a dynasty noted by novelist Edith Wharton for its "barbarous customs but sensuous refinements". The 66 royal tombs that are housed here date from the late 16th and early 17th centuries, but were unknown to the outside world until the 1920s, when they were revealed by the curiosity of a French official. The complex may be modest in size but it is beautifully decorated in the Alhambran style with plenty of carved cedar, stucco and polychromic tiling. The tombs have three main burial chambers that are ranged around a small garden.

Ornate doorways

This is a very small site, easily crowded by the presence of just a single tour group. Visit early morning or late afternoon for the best chance of avoiding the crush.

The Sultana Hotel *(see p116)* next door has a good rooftop terrace restaurant open to the public for lunch and dinner.

- *Map J6*
- *Saadian Tombs: Rue de la Kasbah, Medina; Open 8:30–11:45am, 2:30–5pm daily; Adm 10 Dh*
- *Centre Artisanal: 7 derb Baissi Kasbah, off Rue de la Kasbah; 0524 38 18 53; Open 8:30am–8pm daily; MC, V accepted*

Top 10 Features

1. Saadian Dynasty
2. Entranceway
3. Prayer Hall
4. Hall of Twelve Columns
5. Main Chamber
6. The Garden
7. Kasbah Mosque
8. Morning Market
9. Rue de la Kasbah
10. Centre Artisanal

1 Saadian Dynasty (1549–1668)

Setting out from their powerbase in Taroudant, to the south of the Atlas Mountains, the Saadians defeated the ruling Merenids of Fès. Having established their court at Marrakech, they revitalized the city, endowing it with grand monuments. They were in power for less than 120 years.

2 Entranceway

Reached via the narrowest of twisting passageways *(above)*, the tombs remained a closely guarded secret for centuries. Even today, visiting retains an element of discovery for tourists.

Main Chamber

3 Prayer Hall

The first chamber, intended as a place of prayer, now contains tombs. Most of them are not from the Saadian era, but date back to the Alaouite rulers' era.

4 Hall of Twelve Columns

This chamber holds the tombs of the Sultan Ahmed El Mansour, along with his entire family *(right)*. The stele is in finely worked cedar wood and stuccowork. The graves are beautifully designed and made from the striking Carrara marble that is particular to Italy.

5 Main Chamber

A grand pavilion at the garden's centre is the only real bit of architecture in the complex. A tall, green-tiled, roofed structure in the Andalusian style, it has three soaring portals with beautiful carved wood and a stucco frieze of eight-pointed stars. Housed within are more mosaic-covered tombs.

6 The Garden

The serene garden has countless headstones dotted among the bushes and scrubby plants. These mark the tombs of several children, plus guards and servants. The garden is hugely popular with the local community of stray cats.

7 Kasbah Mosque

Pre-dating the tombs by around 400 years, this mosque was originally built in the year 1190. Since then it has undergone a number of renovations. The cut-brick on green-tile background that decorates the minaret, however, dates back to its original construction.

8 Morning Market

A small square formed by the convergence of several small side streets south of the tombs is host to a modest fruit and vegetable market every morning except Fridays. Take the second left as you walk south from the tombs to this covered street.

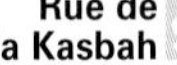

9 Rue de la Kasbah

When you exit the tombs, take a left to reach this main street running through the old kasbah quarter. It runs arrow straight down towards the Grand Méchouar, or what is known as the parade ground of the royal palace.

10 Centre Artisanal

One of two vast, government-run stores selling Moroccan handicrafts, it's a one-stop opportunity to stock up on kaftans, jewellery, carpets and ceramics, all at fixed prices. Ideal for anyone who dislikes the hassle of haggling in the souk.

Islamic burials

In Islam, it is customary to begin the burial process within 24 hours of death. After a ritual washing, the body of the deceased is wrapped in a funeral shroud. It is then put directly into the ground, laid on its right side and facing Mecca. Graves are raised to prevent anyone from sitting or walking on them. Islam forbids cremation.

TOP 10 Medersa Ben Youssef

It is not the oldest or most significant of Marrakech monuments, but the medersa is one of the city's most impressive buildings and allows entry to non-Muslims. It was built by the Saadian sultan, Moulay Abdellah, around 1565, and was rebuilt in the 16th century. It displays all the fine decorative detailing that characterizes what was the golden age of Moroccan architecture. The medersa has also had a brush with movie stardom, as an Algerian Sufi retreat in the Kate Winslet movie Hideous Kinky.

Arches at entrance

Architectural detail

You can get a ticket that combines visits to the medersa, Musée de Marrakech and Koubba El Badiyin *(see p68).*

The neighbouring Musée de Marrakech *(see p68)* has a small café selling snacks and drinks.

- *Map K2*
- *Fondation Omar Benjelloun, Place Ben Youssef, Medina*
- *0524 39 09 11*
- *Open Apr–Sep 9am–7pm daily, Oct–Mar 9am–6pm daily (except during religious holidays)*
- *Adm 40 Dh; combined ticket to visit Musée de Marrakech and Koubba El Badiyin 60 Dh, discount 8–18 years, under-8 years free*
- *www.musee.ma*
- *musee.de.marrakech@menara.ma*

Top 10 Features

1. Ablutions Basin
2. Main Courtyard
3. Tiling
4. Carved stucco
5. Prayer Hall
6. The role of the medersa
7. Dar Bellarj
8. Student Cells
9. Chrob ou Chouf Fountain
10. Rue du Souk des Fassis

1 Ablutions Basin

The entrance is via a long, dark corridor leading to a square vestibule opening into a large courtyard. On the left is a marble basin carved with floral motifs in the Andalusian style.

2 Main Courtyard

At the heart of the medersa is a light-filled courtyard with arcades down two sides, a rectangular pool in the middle and a prayer hall. Every surface has some decoration.

3 Tiling

The lowest part of the courtyard walls is covered with *zellij* (glazed tiles) tiling in an eight-pointed star motif *(below)*. Above this is a band of stylized Koranic text that is interwoven with floral designs.

4 Carved stucco

Vertical panels of intricately carved plaster stretching above the tiling are decorated with inscriptions or geometric patterns *(below)*; depiction of humans or animals is prohibited by Islam.

5 Prayer Hall

The elaborately decorated prayer hall has an octagonal wooden-domed roof supported by marble columns. The stucco features rare palm motifs and calligraphy of Koranic texts. The room is well-lit by openwork gypsum windows which are crowned by stalactite cupolas.

6 The role of the medersa

A medersa was a place for religious instruction – a theological college. The students who boarded here would have studied the Koran and discussed it with the institute's *fqih* or imam (learned religious figures).

7 Dar Bellarj

To the north of the medersa's entrance, Dar Bellarj is a former stork hospital (the name means "House of the Storks"). The building now houses a temporary film school, Ecole Supérieure des Arts Visuels de Marrakech.

8 Student Cells

Arranged on two levels around the central courtyard *(right)* are 130 tiny rooms. Much like monks' cells, nearly 900 students from Muslim countries studied here until the medersa fell out of use in the 1960s.

9 Chrob ou Chouf Fountain

A twist and turn north of the medersa, this handsome fountain (its name means "drink and look") is worth seeking out. A big cedar lintel covered in calligraphy *(below)*, it is a relic of a time when it was a pious act to provide a public source of clean drinking water.

10 Rue du Souk des Fassis

This wriggling alley to the medersa's east is lined by beautifully restored fondouks or old hostels. Some are now centres for artisans. One is a fine restaurant, Le Foundouk.

Ben Youssef Mosque

The medersa, in its earlier days, was part of the complex of the nearby Almoravid mosque which was founded by Ali Ben Youssef during his reign between 1106–42, to which it was once attached. For several centuries, this mosque was the focal point of worship in the medina, and together with the medersa it constituted an important centre of the Islamic religion in the country.

For more information on fondouks, **see pp15 and 67,** *and for Le Foundouk restaurant,* **see p71.**

TOP 10 Badii Palace

It reputedly took armies of labourers and craftsmen 25 years to complete the Badii Palace. When it was finished, it was said to be among the most magnificent palaces ever constructed, with walls and ceilings encrusted with gold and a massive pool with an island flanked by four sunken gardens. This grand folly survived for all of a century before another conquering sultan came along and stripped the place bare (a procedure that itself took 12 years) and carted the riches to his new capital at Meknès. All that survives today are the denuded mudbrick ruins.

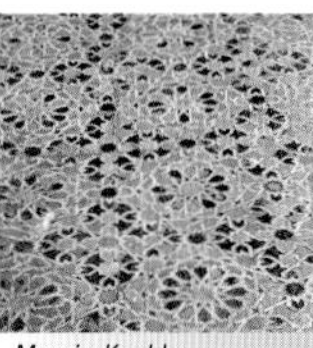

Mosaic, Koubba El Khamsiniya

It's a big sight with very little shelter, so avoid visiting in the heat of the afternoon. It's a good idea to bring some bottled water.

The rooftop terrace of the Kozybar *(see p65)* on Place des Ferblantiers is the perfect vantage point for a bird's-eye view of the palace walls and the storks that nest upon it.

- *Map K5*
- *Place des Ferblantiers, Medina*
- *Open 8:45–11:45am, 2:30–5:45pm daily*
- *Adm 10 Dh; an additional 10 Dh for entry to the Koutoubia minbar pavilion*

Top 10 Features

1. Sultan Ahmed El Mansour
2. The gatehouse
3. Basins and gardens
4. A sinister omen
5. Pavilion of 50 Columns
6. Mosque minbar
7. Underground passages
8. Rooftop terrace
9. Storks
10. Khaysuran Pavilion

1 Sultan Ahmed El Mansour

The palace was built by Ahmed El Mansour, who became sultan after the Battle of Three Kings (1578), in which the Moroccans vanquished the Portuguese. Great wealth was accrued from the ransom of Portuguese captives and from further successful campaigns in Mali. These riches were poured into building the Badii Palace.

Koubba El Khamsiniya and basins

2 The gatehouse

The palace is approached along a narrow way between twin high walls *(below)*. On its completion, the gatehouse carried an inscription to the glories of the palace. Now it is a ruin and entry to the complex is through a breach in the crumbling walls.

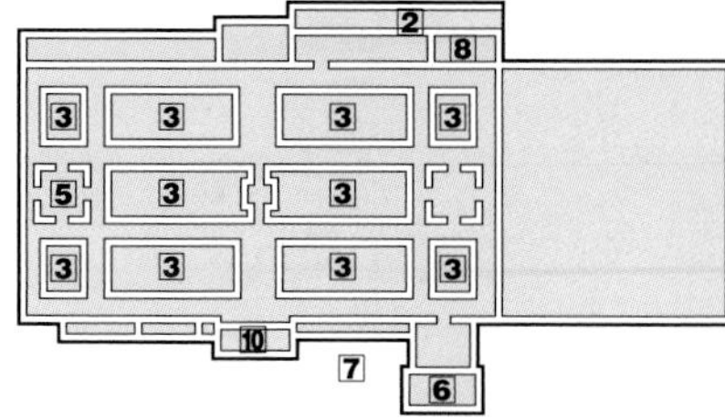

3 Basins & gardens

The palace's central courtyard is dominated by five basins and four sunken gardens planted with orange trees. Of the five basins, the central one has an island that comes alive every July for the Festival of Popular Arts. It is also used as a venue during the International Film Festival *(see p44)*.

4 A sinister omen

At a banquet to celebrate the palace's completion, a guest declared, "When it is demolished, it will make a fine ruin." El Mansour was rendered speechless; the guest's sinister omen has come true.

5 Pavilion of 50 Columns

Ruins around the sides of the courtyard were probably summer houses. The Koubba El Khamsiniya on the far western side is named after the 50 pillars used in its construction.

6 Mosque minbar

An "annexe du palais" in the southeast corner displays the 12th-century pulpit *(minbar)* from Koutoubia Mosque. Intricately carved, this is a celebrated work of art of Moorish Spain.

7 Underground passages

Beside the annexe, a path leads down into the former stables and dungeon *(above)*. Though you can enter, the chambers are only partially lit.

8 Rooftop terrace

At the northeastern corner is the only intact tower with an internal staircase to the roof where it's possible to get a sense of the immense size of the complex.

9 Storks

The protrusions in the crumbling walls are well-loved by city storks who have made their nests here. Considered holy, an old Berber belief has it that storks are actually transformed humans.

10 Khaysuran Pavilion

A pavilion on the north of the great court, once the palace harem, now serves as an exhibition hall with shows of work by local and locally based foreign artists.

The Battle of the Three Kings

In an attempt to wrest the throne from his uncle, Abdel Malek, the Saadian Abu Abdallah Mohammed II, along with King Sebastian of Portugal, declared war. Fought in the town of Ksar El Kebir, between Tangier and Fès, all three died in the battle. Malek was succeeded by his brother, Ahmed El Mansour, builder of the Badii Palace.

For more information on the Koutoubia Mosque, **see pp12–13.**

Majorelle Gardens

Of Marrakech's numerous gardens (see pp42–3), *these are the most famous and the legacy of an expatriate French painter, Jacques Majorelle, who considered himself a "gardenist". In 1924, he acquired land and set about creating a botanical sanctuary around his studio. Majorelle opened his gardens to the public in 1947 and they remained a popular attraction until his death 15 years later. The property fell into disrepair until 1980, when it was rescued from ruin by French fashion designer Yves Saint-Laurent and his artist-friend Pierre Bergé.*

Flowering cactus

A painted pot

This is another very small site, easily crowded by the presence of just a single tour group. Visit early morning or late afternoon for the best chance of avoiding the crush.

There is a small, expensive café in the gardens, open from 8am, serving hot and cold drinks, salads, sandwiches and, until 11:30am, three kinds of breakfast.

* *Map C4*
* *Avenue Yacoub El Mansour, Guéliz*
* *0524 31 30 47*
* *Open daily: Oct–May 8am–5:30pm; Jun–Sep 8am–6pm; Ramadan 9am–5pm*
* *Adm to gardens 30 Dh; Museum of Islamic Art 15 Dh*
* *www.jardinmajorelle.com*

Top 10 Features

1. Jacques Majorelle
2. Louis Majorelle
3. The plants
4. *Bassins* and fountains
5. Boutique
6. Islamic Art Museum
7. Doors and ceilings
8. Majorelle's paintings
9. Majorelle blue
10. Petrol station

1 Jacques Majorelle

French artist Jacques Majorelle (1886–1962) came to Marrakech in 1919 to recuperate from his heart problems and immediately saw the painterly potential of southern Morocco.

2 Louis Majorelle

Louis Majorelle was the painter's equally famous father. A French decorator and furniture designer, he was one of the leading exponents of the Art Nouveau style. His work is displayed in celebrated museums, such as the Musée d'Orsay in Paris.

3 The plants

A beautiful bamboo "forest" and an arid cactus garden with species from around the world share garden space *(below)*. Most stunning of all are the flowering masses of red and purple bougainvillea.

Situated northwest of the medina in the New City, it's a good idea to take a taxi or calèche *to the gardens,* **see p104**.

4 *Bassins* and fountains

The garden has a fountain and two large *bassins* or pools *(left)*, the smaller fed by a sloping channel. Next to the museum, a third pool is filled with golden carp.

5 Boutique

In the northeast corner, a small boutique sells an interesting array of quality local handicrafts including clothing, jewellery and miscellaneous leather products such as bags, sandals and beautifully bound notebooks. However, there is a notable paucity of information concerning Majorelle and his garden.

6 Islamic Art Museum

The painter's former studio now houses a well-presented exhibition on Berber culture, which includes Berber jewellery, fine embroidery and carved wooden items.

7 Doors and ceilings

Arguably the highlight of the museum is its collection of wooden doors and ceilings *(below)*, all beautifully carved. Some of the ceiling panels are painted but most impressive are the huge double doors dating from the 17th to the 19th centuries.

8 Majorelle's paintings

The museum's first room has a series of lithographs depicting various Atlas kasbahs. Some of Majorelle's most acclaimed works were the tourism posters that he created for Morocco.

9 Majorelle blue

The name Majorelle lives on in an electrifying shade of cobalt blue – known as "Majorelle blue" – that is widely used in the garden. The artist's former studio is also painted in this colour.

10 Galerie Love

Yves Saint Laurent's "LOVE" posters, created using collage and sent yearly as New Year's greetings to fashionable friends and clients, are exhibited here.

Yves Saint-Laurent

French designer Yves Saint-Laurent first visited the city in 1962. By the end of the 1960s, he'd bought his first house here. Later, he moved into a villa next to Majorelle Gardens, which he purchased and saved from being destroyed to make way for an apartment complex. After his death a small memorial stone was placed in the gardens, which now belong to a trust to ensure their continued upkeep.

TOP 10 Mamounia Hotel

One of the world's great old hotels, since opening in 1923 the Mamounia has been welcoming the rich and famous; Winston Churchill was one of the most celebrated guests to have frequented this hotel. It was originally built in the 19th century as the palace of the crown prince of Morocco, but in 1923 the French turned it into a hotel for the Moroccan railways. It is set within 7 hectares (17 acres) of delightful gardens surrounded by the city's 12th-century red ochre ramparts.

Restaurant interior

Non-guests wishing to visit the Mamounia should dress smartly – people wearing shorts and T-shirts are generally not allowed to enter.

The hotel boasts several bars and restaurants but perhaps the most pleasurable experience can be had at the lunchtime buffet served beside the swimming pool in the gardens.

- *Map H5*
- *Avenue Bab Jedid, Medina*
- *0524 38 86 00*
- *The gardens: Open 24 hours; non-guests allowed*
- *resa@mamounia.com*
- *www.mamounia.com*

Top 10 Features

1. The rooms
2. The gardens
3. Guestbook
4. The suites
5. Majorelle Ceiling
6. Winston Churchill
7. Churchill's paintings
8. The architects
9. The Man Who Knew Too Much
10. The birds

1 The rooms

Many of the rooms in this landmark hotel have been luxuriously renovated using wood and leather in warm Moroccan shades.

2 The gardens

The acres of formal European-style gardens were laid out for the prince and pre-date the construction of the hotel. Well-manicured paths lead between ponds and flower-beds to a central pavilion.

Mamounia Hotel

3 Guestbook

Sean Connery and Catherine Deneuve, Bill Clinton, plus scribbles from Kate Winslet and Will Smith: Mamounia's *livre d'or* must be among the starriest guestbooks.

4 The suites

Among its several grand suites, the most famous is the one named after Winston Churchill *(below)*. The decoration is intended to evoke the era when the politician visited and contains artifacts including his pipe.

5 Majorelle Ceiling

Winston Churchill met fellow painter Jacques Majorelle *(see pp26–7)* in 1946 during one of his stays at the Mamounia. The portly politician persuaded the hotel's management to commission a mural by Majorelle *(above)*, which you can now see on the ceiling of the extended lobby.

6 Winston Churchill

"This is a wonderful place, and the hotel one of the best I have ever used," were Churchill's views on the hotel and the city that he adored, in a letter to his wife, Clementine.

7 Churchill's paintings

Churchill would paint in the afternoon and was fond of Marrakech's extraordinary light. A couple of his paintings still hang in the hotel.

8 The architects

The original architects of the Mamounia blended art deco with traditional Moroccan motifs *(left)*. In 1986, renovations were carried out by the designers of Morocco's royal palaces, further changing the character of the building.

9 The Man Who Knew Too Much

Several scenes of this 1956 Alfred Hitchcock thriller *(below)*, with James Stewart and Doris Day, were shot in the hotel.

10 The birds

The story may be apocryphal, but film director Alfred Hitchcock was supposedly inspired to make his movie *The Birds* after being dive-bombed by finches on his balcony at the Mamounia.

If you'd like to stay at the hotel, **see p116.**

The Lord of the Atlas, Thami El Glaoui

Top 10 Moments in History

1 Founding of Marrakech
The Almoravids, the most powerful Berber tribe, founded the military outpost of Marra Kouch in 1062, giving them control of the Saharan trade routes.

2 The Almohads take Marrakech
The Almohads lay siege to Marrakech in 1147 and the city changed hands. Their impressive monuments, including the Koutoubia Mosque, dominate Marrakech to this day.

Portrait of King Mohammed V

3 Decline under the Merenids
Emerging from eastern Morocco, the Merenids took the city from the weakening Almohads in 1269. During their rule, Marrakech was sidelined and reduced to a provincial outpost after they chose the northerly city of Fès as their power base.

4 The Saadians return the throne to Marrakech
Prosperity returned to Marrakech under the Saadians, who overthrew the Merenids in 1549. This first Arab dynasty expanded their territory across the Sahara to Mali and Mauritania.

5 Moulay Ismail
The Saadians were swept aside by the Alaouites in 1668. Their second ruler, Moulay Ismail, was noted as much for his cruelty as for his diplomacy skills. He reigned for 55 years. The Alaouite dynasty still rules today.

6 The Sultan of Spliff
Moulay Hassan, a powerful sultan who ruled from 1873–94, legalised cannabis cultivation. Today the Rif region is one of the world's largest cultivators, even though measures have been taken in an effort to eradicate this.

The mosque at Tin Mal, built by the Almohads

7 Imposition of French rule
The lynching of Europeans in Casablanca gave

Preceding pages **Menara Gardens**

France an excuse to implement her territorial ambitions. The consequent March 1912 Treaty of Fès made Morocco France's protectorate. In this period, a whole *nouvelle ville* (new city) was constructed outside the walls of the medina.

8 The Lord of the Atlas

The French enlisted tribal warlord Thami El Glaoui to rule southern Morocco from 1918–55. The self-styled "Lord of the Atlas", known for his cruel ways, ruled the city with an iron fist. After the French withdrawal in 1955, El Glaoui fell into disgrace.

9 The crowning of the king

1955 marked the return of exiled Sultan Mohammed V who was crowned king, with Morocco gaining independence a year later. The present monarch, Mohammed VI, is his grandson.

10 Marrakech goes global

It is claimed that a French television programme in the 1990s, stating that a palace in Marrakech could be bought for the price of a flat in Paris, was the catalyst for the city's new-found popularity. Five-star hotels and budget airlines soon followed suit.

Signing the Treaty of Fès

Top 10 Chronicles of Morocco

1 Travels of Ibn Battuta (14th century)

This famous Islamic voyager travelled as far as China. He regarded Marrakech as "one of the most beautiful cities".

2 Adventures in Morocco (1874)

An account by German Gerhard Rohlfs, who travelled North Africa as a vagabond.

3 Mogreb-El-Aksa (1897)

Robert Cunninghame Graham, former Scottish member of parliament, tried to reach Taroudant disguised as a Muslim sheikh.

4 In Morocco (1920)

A visit to Morocco and Marrakech in 1917 inspired novelist Edith Wharton to try her hand at travel writing.

5 Morocco That Was (1921)

An entertaining account (especially of the Moroccan royalty) by *Times* correspondent Walter Harris.

6 A Year in Marrakech (1953)

Peter Mayne's engaging journal of a city little changed since medieval times.

7 Lords of the Atlas (1966)

A history of the colourful Glaoui era by Gavin Maxwell.

8 Hideous Kinky (1992)

Emma Freud's humourous account of a dysfunctional 1970s childhood in Marrakech.

9 The Tangier Diaries (1997)

An account by John Hopkins of 1950s Tangier with drug-fuelled forays to Marrakech.

10 The Red City (2003)

A collection of writings on Marrakech down the ages.

Left **Painting by Winston Churchill** Right **Actor Colin Farrell in Oliver Stone's *Alexander***

Top 10 Celebrity Visitors

1 Winston Churchill
Between 1935–59, British Prime Minister Winston Churchill visited Marrakech no less than six times. "It is," he reportedly said, "the most lovely spot in the world." Usually at the Mamounia Hotel *(see pp28–9)*, his mornings were spent penning his memoirs and afternoons were devoted to painting, his favourite hobby.

2 George Orwell
The famous author of *Animal Farm* and *1984* was in Marrakech in 1939 on the advice of his doctor (Orwell suffered from tuberculosis). While recuperating, he wrote *Coming Up for Air* and an essay, "Marrakech".

3 The Rolling Stones
Brian Jones of the Rolling Stones visited Marrakech in 1966 and brought the rest of the band on the next trip. Put up at the Hotel Es Saadi in Hivernage, they bumped into Cecil Beaton, who photographed Mick Jagger and Keith Richards by the pool.

4 Yves Saint-Laurent
The French couturier first visited the Red City in 1962 when memories of his childhood in Oran, Algeria were reignited. He returned a few years later and bought a house in the medina. The city found its way into his work as well, with the colours and patterns of southern Morocco influencing his collections. He spent part of the year here in a villa adjacent to the Majorelle Gardens *(see pp26–7)*.

5 Colin Farrell
Southern Morocco has long been favoured by Hollywood as an exotic, versatile and, most importantly, cheap spot for filming. Consequently, Marrakech has become a favourite place for actors to unwind; while shooting for *Alexander*, actor Colin Farrell reputedly ran up a $64,000 hotel bill at Le Méridien N'Fis.

6 P. Diddy
In 2002, rap artist P. Diddy flew nearly 300 guests into Marrakech on chartered jets from New York and Paris to celebrate his 33rd birthday in opulent Moroccan style. The king, apparently a rap fan, also contributed to the party and lent him the use of the Bahia Palace *(see p63)* for the high-profile celebrations.

P. Diddy's birthday celebrations in Marrakech

For information on the Atlas Corporation Studio in Ouarzazate, home to the Moroccan film industry, **see p97.**

Charles de Gaulle and Winston Churchill

7 **John Paul Getty Jr.**
In the 1960s, American oil heir John Paul Getty Jr. and his wife Talitha owned a place in the medina. They were famously photographed by Patrick Lichfield clad in kaftans on their mansion's roof terrace with a backdrop of the Atlas Mountains.

8 **Paul Bowles**
The author of *The Sheltering Sky* was an occasional visitor to Marrakech. There's a famous photograph of him from 1961, taken while he was sitting on the roof terrace of the Café Glacier.

9 **General Charles de Gaulle**
After the Casablanca Conference in January 1943, a meeting of leaders of the Allied forces, General Charles de Gaulle travelled to Marrakech, staying at the Mamounia Hotel. The hotel's director had to create a bed for him in order to accommodate his considerable frame.

10 **Robert Plant**
Led Zeppelin vocalist Robert Plant and guitarist Jimmy Page first visited Marrakech in 1975. Twenty years later, they recorded some video footage on Jemaa El Fna to accompany the release of their album "No Quarter".

Morocco on Film

1 **Othello (1952)**
Orson Welles put the Moor in Morocco, shooting much of his troubled masterpiece in Essaouira.

2 **The Man Who Knew Too Much (1955)**
Hitchcock filmed James Stewart and Doris Day in the Mamounia and Jemaa El Fna.

3 **Our Man in Marrakech (1966)**
A little-seen silly spy comedy, but the city features heavily.

4 **Kundun (1997)**
The Atlas Mountains were cast as Tibet in this Scorsese epic. Some of the film's props can still be seen at Kasbah du Toubkal *(see p56)*.

5 **Hideous Kinky (1998)**
The souks and Jemaa El Fna were prominent in this film adaptation of Emma Freud's autobiographical book.

6 **Gladiator (2000)**
Russell Crowe is sold into slavery at Aït Benhaddou *(see p95)*. Also shot here were *The Last Temptation of Christ* and *Lawrence of Arabia*.

7 **Black Hawk Down (2001)**
US marines, caught in a firefight in Somalia, did all their shooting in Morocco.

8 **Alexander (2004)**
Alexander of Macedonia was, in fact, Alexander of Marrakech.

9 **Babel (2006)**
The village of Tazatine in southern Morocco appears as itself in this film.

10 **Prince of Persia: The Sands of Time (2010)**
Filmed near Marrakech, Jake Gyllenhaal stars in this action adventure based on a popular video game.

For more on Essaouira, favoured Hollywood destination in Morocco, **see pp80–83.**

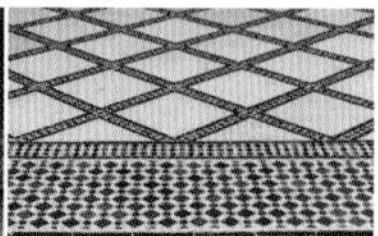

Left and centre **Details of the courtyard in Hotel La Sultana** Right **The Bahia Palace courtyard**

TOP 10 Moroccan Architecture

1 Horseshoe arches

Properly known as outrepassé arches, these are where the arch curves back inwards after its widest point, to give an effect like a horseshoe or keyhole. Its use is most commonly associated with Moorish Spain and North Africa.

2 *Zellij* tiling

One of the most striking features of Moroccan architecture is its use of multi-coloured, small tiles laid in complex geometric patterns. This is known as the *zellij* technique, where tiles are created as large squares and then hand cut into smaller shapes. Conventional shapes and sizes are typically used, though there are as many as 360 different types of pieces.

3 *Tadelakt* plaster

This technique was initially associated only with bathhouses to counter the heat and moisture. Walls are treated with a plaster of powdered limestone, which, once set, is polished with flat stones, then painted with a glaze of egg whites and polished again with the local black soap, made from olives. The finished surface looks akin to soft leather.

4 Stucco plaster

A decorative element of Moroccan architecture, carved plaster can cover entire walls in fantastic curvilinear and geometric design. The work is executed by craftsmen while the plaster is still damp – the patterns are sketched onto the surface, then gouged out with hammer and chisel.

5 Carved woodwork

Although some of the same designs are used to decorate both plaster and wood, often wood is deployed as a frieze and carries inscriptions in Arabic, the language in which the Koran was revealed to the Prophet Mohammed and therefore of a sacred character. The inscriptions are of a religious nature and invariably praise the glory of Allah. They are used both to decorate and impart information.

Horseshoe arch, Medersa Ben Youssef

6 Square minarets

The square design of Moroccan minarets can be traced to the Umayyad rulers of Islamic Spain, who were of Syrian origin. Syrians are almost unique in the Middle East for their square minarets, probably influenced by the church towers built by Syrian Christians.

Exterior of Koubba El Badiyin

7 Courtyards
A distinctive feature of Islamic architecture is its focus on internal spaces as opposed to the exterior, where the façades are generally ordinary windowless walls. Courtyards serve as air-wells into which the cool night air sinks. They also allow women to venture outside while shielding them from the eyes of strange men.

8 Fountains
Fountains and basins are required for ritual ablutions before prayers. Also, in an arid climate, the provision of drinking water is seen as a charitable act.

9 Pisé
The basic building material used in Morocco, *pisé* is wet earth mixed with straw and gravel pounded between two parallel boards and strengthened by lime. If not well made, the structure can crumble in the rain – Southern Morocco is littered with semi-melted buildings.

10 Pigeonholes
The numerous pigeonholes peppering walls in the city are, in reality, remnants of wooden scaffolding used to erect walls.

Top 10 Historic Buildings

1 Koubba El Badiyin
The earliest example of Islamic architecture with beautiful carved plasterwork seen nowhere else in Morocco *(see p68)*.

2 Koutoubia Mosque
The city's biggest and tallest minaret *(see pp12–13)*.

3 Badii Palace
Its *pisé* walls are in an advanced state of dilapidation with clearly visible "pigeonholes" *(see pp24–5)*.

4 Bahia Palace
This 19th-century palace features a riot of *zellij* work *(see p62)*.

5 Medersa Ben Youssef
This structure displays nearly all the decorative elements, including fine *zellij* work, superbly carved stucco and woodwork *(see pp22–3)*.

6 Tin Mal Mosque
Some rare, surviving carved plasterwork dating to the early Almohad dynasty adorns the interiors *(see p90)*.

7 Bab Agnaou
This gate into the kasbah quarter is in the form of a keyhole arch *(see p18)*.

8 Dar Cherifa
Home to a busy cultural centre, this is an example of a wealthy courtyard home, with some extraordinary carved woodwork *(see p67)*.

9 Dar El Bacha
Enough dazzling multi-coloured, polychromically-patterned *zellij* tiling to make your head spin *(see p69)*.

10 Dar Si Said
For an insight into architectural techniques and decoration, visit this museum *(see pp62–3)*.

Left **A Bill Willis-designed fireplace at Dar Yacout** Right **Palais Rhoul with its trendy domes**

TOP 10 Modern Moroccan Styles

1 Coloured *tadelakt*

Traditionally, this silky plaster finish with its water-resistant qualities *(see p36)* was reserved for bathhouses, but interior designers have now begun applying it for all sorts of rooms. The range of colours has also broadened; now it's common to see *tadelakt* in pink, green or even black.

2 Bill Willis

Willis, a Tennessee-born designer, first accompanied Paul Getty Jr. *(see p35)* to Marrakech in 1968. He worked on the Getty house, then designed one for the Rothschilds and another for Yves Saint-Laurent *(see pp26–7 & 34)*. Willis lived in Marrakech until his death in 2009 and was enormously influential in the reinterpretation of traditional Moroccan crafts and styles for the modern age.

Carved plaster, Riad Farnatchi

3 Mud-hut chic

The term was coined by style magazines and refers to a new generation of highly designed buildings that advance the art of constructing in *pisé (see p37)*. They enhance traditional forms by adding vibrant colours and cool, modern decorative touches.

4 Lanterns

One of the essentials of any modern Moroccan riad is an ostentatious lantern. Known in Arabic as *fanous (see p16)*, these large lanterns are fashioned from beaten metal laced with cut-out patterns, and they have historically been connected with the celebrations for Ramadan. One whole area of the souks has been given over to their manufacture.

5 Modern *zellij*

The traditional art of laying *zellij (see p36)* has evolved over time in new and exciting ways. Contemporary designers use unusual colours and striking colour combinations. Earlier limited to wainscoting, *zelije* is now applied to a greater variety of surfaces.

6 Charles Boccara

Born in Tunisia, educated in Morocco and professionally trained in France, Boccara is an influential Marrakech architect. He was one of the first to take traditional Moroccan elements

Mud-hut chic at Hotel Caravanserai

and reinterpret them to suit the modern age. He has often been credited with repopularising *tadelakt* and domes.

7 Beaten copper

Wafer-thin coverings of beaten metal, earlier adorning grand wooden doors, are now used to fashion sheets of copper into hand basins.

8 Stucco madness

With updated traditional techniques, the interiors have made creative use of carved plaster, like the floor-to-ceiling stucco of the dining room at Riad Farnatchi *(see left & p116)*, which resembles flock wallpaper.

9 Fretwork

Moroccan craftsmen are adept at transforming ordinary sheets into geometric-patterned screens and furniture panels, which are sometimes backlit to stunning effect. Although not indigenous to the country, they also assemble small, lathe-turned pieces of wood to form the screens known as *mashrabiya*.

10 Colour

While Marrakech is a uniform dusky pink, her interiors are painted in bold colours. Favourites are fruity orange, rose pink, lemon yellow, mustard and cobalt sky blue.

Top 10 Milestones in Modern Moroccan Styles

1 Jnane Tamsna
An elegant Palmeraie villa which is a regular venue for fashion shoots *(see p117)*.

2 Tichka Salam Hotel
Look out for Bill Willis' palm tree columns in the restaurant *(see p111)*.

3 Les Deux Tours
A landmark design by Charles Boccara with plenty of *tadelakt* and mud-brick domes *(see p117)*.

4 Riad Enija
A conversion of old townhouses updated and filled with fabulous custom-made furniture *(see p116)*.

5 Théâtre Royal
A spectacular Boccara building on a monumental scale *(see p76)*.

6 Dar Yacout
More Willis magic at work, including magnificent candy-striped fireplaces *(see p71)*.

7 Riad Kaiss
A modest riad with contemporary Moroccan design by French architect Christian Ferré *(see p114)*.

8 Amanjena
This vast luxury hotel is modern Moroccan as an operatic set piece, complete with reservoirs and green tile-roofed pavilions *(see p117)*.

9 Dar Les Cigognes
A Charles Boccara, it typically features gorgeous *tadelakt*, plus beautiful wood and plaster carvings.

10 Le Foundouk
This restaurant combines the traditional (a courtyard building) with the modern (backlit water features, a bar) to sublime effect *(see p71)*.

To buy your own piece of Marrakech style, **see pp16–17.**

Products used in Moroccan *hammams* and spas

Hammams and Spas

1 Hammam El Bacha

One of the most historic *hammams*, it was initially used by the staff of the Dar El Bacha *(see p69)* just across the road. Still functioning, though poorly maintained, the highlight is an impressive 6-m (20-foot) cupola in the steam room. *Map H3 • 20 rue Fatima Zohra, Medina • Open: men 7am–1pm daily; women 1–9pm daily • No credit cards*

2 Hammam Etiquette

All *hammams* are single sex and have three main rooms: one cool, one hot, one – the steam room – very hot. Men keep on their underwear, women go naked. In public *hammams*, a masseur is available for an additional fee. Carry your own towels and toiletries.

3 La Maison Arabe

The *hammams* housed in larger riads and hotels are often restricted to guests, but not at the Maison Arabe. Book yourself in for a vigorous *gommage* (rubdown) with a *kissa* (loofah mitten) and follow it up with a thorough massage. *Map H2 • 1 derb Assehbe, Bab Doukkala • 0524 38 70 10 • Open 11am–7pm daily; by appt • www.lamaisonarabe.com • MC, V accepted*

4 Palais Rhoul

The *hammam* is attached to an exclusive Palmeraie villa *(see p117)* but is open to all. Purpose-built, it is palatial, with a central plunge pool. *Dar Tounisi Km 5, Route de Fès, Palmeraie • 0524 32 94 94 • Open 9:30am–7pm daily; by appt only • www.palais-rhoul.com • MC, V accepted*

Cut-glass bottle

5 Massage

All riads offer massages on request, but for a professional touch, visit a *hammam* or go to one of the spas burgeoning in the city. Most local masseurs use essential oils, including locally produced argan oil *(see p90)*. Some also specialize in particular techniques such as *tuina* or deep touch.

6 Bains de Marrakech

This spa provides a dazzling selection of treatments, such as water massage, shiatsu and the intriguingly named "four-handed massage". Unusually, the *hammam*

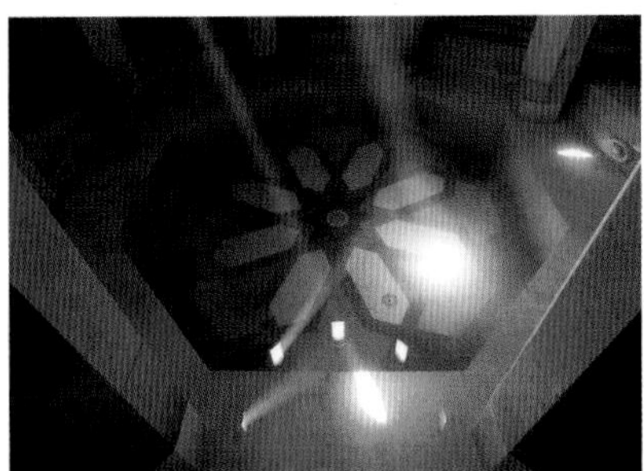

Hammam at Palais Rhoul

Spa jacuzzi at Hotel La Sultana

offers small, mixed steam-bath cubicles (swimsuits compulsory). The adjacent Riad Mehdi is there to quench your thirst after all the exertion. *Map J6 • 2 derb Sedra, Mechouar Bab Agnaou, Kasbah • 0524 38 47 13 • Open 9am–8pm daily • www.riadmehdi.net • Credit cards accepted*

7 La Sultana

A five-star hotel *(see p116)* next to the Saadian Tombs, La Sultana has a beautiful basement spa, complete with a star-domed marble Jacuzzi, a *hammam*, a fitness centre and solarium. Packages include aromatherapy and seaweed treatments. *Map K6 • 403 rue de la Kasbah, Medina • 0524 38 80 08 • Open 10am–8pm daily; closed 6–26 Aug • www.lasultanamarrakech.com • AmEx, MC, V accepted*

8 Hivernage Hotel & Spa

A smart hotel *(see p111)* close to the Mamounia, it has a well-equipped modern spa centre. Services include a *hammam*, essential oil baths, massages and a sports hall for those looking to sweat it out. A sauna, Jacuzzi and a large pool are other options. *Map G4 • Cnr ave Echouhada & rue des Temples, Hivernage • 0524 42 41 00 • Open 9am–10pm daily • www.hivernage-hotel.com • AmEx, MC, V accepted*

9 Hotel Es Saadi

Whether you crave a poolside massage, a traditional cleanse or a space-age experience at the in-house Dior Institut, you are likely to be impressed by the spa facilities at this hotel *(see p111)*. The lavish and stylish decor is worthy of an interiors magazine. *Map C6 • Avenue El Kadissia, Hivernage • 0524 44 88 11 • Open 9am–9pm daily • www.essaadi.com • Credit cards accepted*

10 Hammam Ziani

Located near the Bahia Palace, this *hammam* offers all the basic facilities (scrub, soak, steam and pummel) in significantly cleaner environs than many other medina bathhouses. *Map K4 • Rue Riad Zitoun El Jedid, Medina • 0662 71 55 71 • Open 8am–10pm daily*

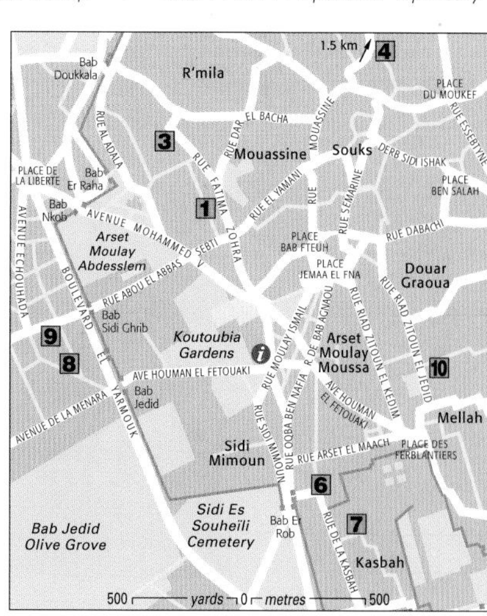

Left **Koutoubia Gardens** Right **Menara Gardens**

Top 10 Parks and Gardens

1 The Palmery

The Beverly Hills of Morocco, the Palmery is a vast palm grove on the northern fringe of the city, and is home to some fantastical and outlandish architectural creations. Some of the luxury villas also double as guesthouses and exclusive hotels *(see p117)*. You can also still see the remains of the early irrigation system introduced by the Almoravids. *Map F4*

2 Menara Gardens

The Menara Gardens, with their orchard, pool and pavilion, epitomize a typical Islamic garden. Laid out in the 12th century, the gardens feature a large pool overlooked by a green tile-roofed pavilion. *Map B7 • Avenue de la Menara, Hivernage • 0524 43 95 80 • Open 5am–6:30pm daily • Free entry; adm to picnic pavilion*

3 Agdal Gardens

Dating back to the 12th century, the Agdal comprises several linked gardens including an orange grove, an olive plantation, vineyards and orchards of pomegranates and figs. The garden was enclosed within *pisé* walls in the 19th century. There is a large pool at its heart called the Tank of Health – in 1873, Sultan Mohammed IV tragically drowned in it when he went boating with his son. Be mindful of pickpockets. *Map E7 • South of the Grand Méchouar • Open Fri, Sun; closed if the king is in residence*

4 Mamounia Gardens

Landscaped with flowerbeds and groves of olives and orange trees, the gardens predate the world-famous Mamounia Hotel. The Arset El Mamoun were established in the 18th century by Prince Moulay Mamoun, laid out around a central pavilion that served as a royal residence; the hotel was added a century later *(see p28)*.

5 Majorelle Gardens

Formerly owned by Yves Saint-Laurent *(see p34)*, the gardens were first created by expatriate French artist Jacques Majorelle. Though small, they are quite lovely, with bamboo groves, cacti and palms, and pools floating with water lilies.

Palm trees, naturally enough, in the Palmery

For more details on the Mamounia Hotel, **see pp28–9.**

Majorelle Gardens

The artist's former studio is now a mini Museum of Islamic Art, painted a searing blue known as "Majorelle blue" *(see pp26–7)*.

6 Arset Moulay Abdesslem

Between Avenue Mohammed V and the walls of the medina, this public garden has been given a makeover. The lawns, divided by palm-shaded pathways, are a favourite lunch spot. The park also has a public Internet centre. *Map G3 • Avenue Mohammed V*

7 Koutoubia Gardens

On the south side of the landmark mosque, these formal gardens have stone pathways lined with flowerbeds and topiary hedges. The roses seem impervious to the heat and appear to be in bloom throughout the year *(see p12)*.

8 Jnane El Harti

It may not be the prettiest, but this neatly planted green space is beloved by locals and its proximity to places of work makes it a favourite lunchtime hangout. Come evening, you will spot young couples looking for a few private moments, away from the prying eyes of families and relatives *(see p77)*.

9 Regreening of Marrakech

Your first pleasant surprise as you drive from the airport are the roads lined with rose bushes and jasmine, all part of an initiative to transform the city into a great green garden.

10 Orange Trees

Apart from jacaranda, the streets of the New City are lined with orange trees which flower and bear fruit each spring. The blossom is sold to perfume companies for use in scents.

Arset Moulay Abdesslem

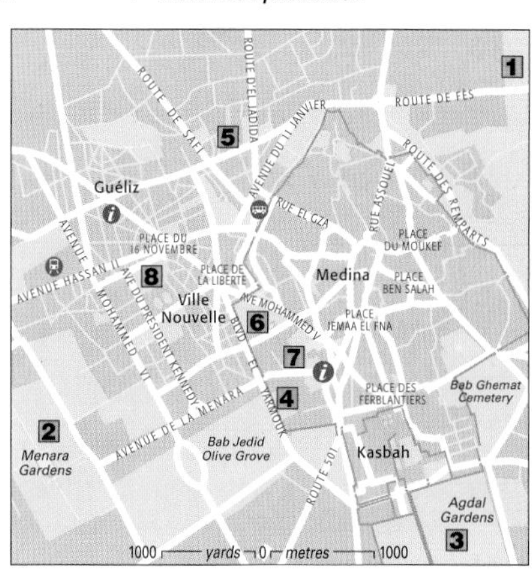

Left **Shelves of books at Café du Livre** Right **Photography exhibition at Galerie 127**

Top 10 Arts and Culture

1 Dar Cherifa

This 16th-century town house is a cultural centre and holds regular exhibitions, often with Gnawa musicians *(see p11)* performing on opening nights. Its small library contains art and heritage books which you can browse through while enjoying some tea or coffee *(see p67)*.

2 Marrakech International Film Festival

Sponsored by movie fan King Mohammed VI, the festival was launched in 2001 and is held in November. Guests who have walked the red carpet include Martin Scorsese and Sean Connery. *www.festival-marrakech.com*

3 Café du Livre

The only place in Marrakech that sells second-hand books in English, the Café du Livre is also a café and restaurant with Wi-Fi. French newspapers and books on Morocco or by Moroccan authors are for sale too *(see pp78–9)*.

4 Festivals in Essaouira

The festival known as Les Musicales d'Essaouira is held in April/May – thousands of classical music lovers enjoy the free concerts and recitals. In June, there is a four-day festival of Gnawa *(see p11)* and world music with two stages reserved for international artists. Impromptu performances are held all over the medina *(see pp80–83)*. *www.festival-gnaoua.net*

5 Galerie 127

Apparently the only gallery in all of North Africa dedicated to photography, its sparse, white-walled room on the second floor exhibits both local and international works. *Map B5 • 127 ave Mohammed V, Guéliz • 0524 43 26 67 • Open 3–7pm Tue–Sat*

6 Arts in Marrakech Festival

Primarily a literary festival, AiM is held the weekend before the international film festival, with art events and exhibitions also featuring. *www.marrakechbiennale.org*

Marrakech International Film Festival

7 Galerie Rê

This is a contemporary art gallery at the northern end of the New City and holds regularly changing exhibitions. The owner, Lucien Viola, a renowned international collector of carpets, also has

For more on films and celebrities, **see pp34–5.**

Berber horse show

plans to open an art museum. Map C5 • Résidence El Andalous III, cnr rue de la Mosquée & rue Ibn Toumert, Guéliz • 0524 43 22 58 • Open 9am–1pm, 3–8pm Mon–Sat. www.galeriere.com

8 **Théâtre Royal**
Created by architect Charles Boccara *(see pp38–9)*, this building is a modern adaptation of traditional Islamic models. Sadly, the 1,200-seat venue is rarely occupied. Nearly 15 years after its design was first undertaken, it remains incomplete but can still be visited *(see p76)*.

9 **Kssour Agafay**
Usually meaning a fortified village, here *kssour* refers to a restored private townhouse in the medina. A private members' club, it opens to the public for Sufi music events, readings and exhibitions. *Map J3 • 52 Sabet Graoua, off rue Mouassine, Medina • 0524 42 70 00 • www.kssouragafay.com*

10 **Marrakech Festival of Popular Arts**
Troupes from all over Morocco perform at this annual celebration of Berber music and dance held in June or July. Don't miss the magnificent *fantasia*, a charge of Berber horsemen, outside the ramparts near the Bab El Jedid. *www.maghrebarts.ma*

Top 10 Moroccan Cultural Figures

1 **Tahar Ben Jelloun**
Morocco's best-known French-based writer won the French Prix Goncourt in 1987 for his novel *The Sacred Night*.

2 **Mahi Binebine**
This Marrakech-based artist authored the excellent *Welcome to Paradise*.

3 **Hassan Haggag**
The graphic artist behind the T-shirts worn by the staff at London's famous Moroccan restaurant, Momo.

4 **Leila Marrakchi**
A Casablanca-born film-maker, her debut feature *Marock* caused a scandal on its release in 2006.

5 **Farid Belkahia**
One of Morocco's most influential artists, he often works on lamb-skin canvases.

6 **Hassan Hakmoun**
Based in New York, this Moroccan trance specialist performed on Jemaa El Fna as a child.

7 **Elie Mouyal**
This well-known architect is high on the list of celebrities looking for a suitably fancy residence.

8 **Master Musicians of Jajouka**
International fame came upon this musical ensemble from a North Moroccan village, courtesy of the Rolling Stones.

9 **Leila Abouzeid**
The first Moroccan woman author to have her work translated into English.

10 **Jamel Debbouze**
Amélie and the Oscar-nominated *Days of Glory* brought this French actor of Moroccan descent into the spotlight.

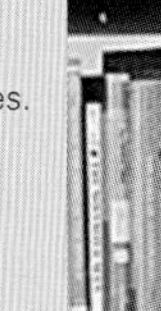

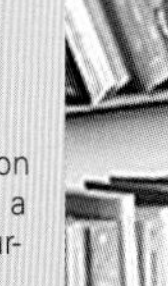

Left **Room at Tchaikana** Right **Suite Berbère at Riyad El Cadi**

TOP 10 Riads

1 Riad El Fenn

El Fenn is a sort of super riad with its four courtyards, two pools, a bar, restaurant, *hammam*, library, cinema screening room and collection of modern art – all shared by just 23 rooms. *Map J3 • 2 derb Moulay Abdallah Ben Hezzian, Bab El Ksour, Medina • 0524 44 12 10 • www.riadelfenn.com •* Dh Dh Dh Dh

2 Riad Farnatchi

The intimate yet deluxe Farnatchi has a design that is a playful update of the local aesthetic. Luxurious suites boast sunken baths and private terraces. *Map K2 • Derb El Farnatchi, off rue Souk des Fassis, Medina • 0524 38 49 10 • www.riadfarnatchi.com •* Dh Dh Dh Dh Dh

3 Riyad El Cadi

This rambling residence, created by connecting no less than seven houses, was designed by a former German ambassador to Morocco with a passion for collecting; the suites, rooms and salons have museum-worthy items of Islamic art, such as wooden screens, Berber hangings and painted ceilings. The riad also has a pool, Jacuzzi, *hammam* and library. *Map K3 • 87 derb Moulay Abdelkader, off derb Debbachi, Medina • 0524 37 86 55 • www.riyadelcadi.com •* Dh Dh Dh

4 Riad Enija

One of the older riads, it still manages to remain one of the most striking. The spacious rooms feature the most outlandish collection of furniture. TV sets, telephones and other modern accoutrements are non-existent, while at the heart of the riad is a wild courtyard garden. *Map K3 • 9 derb Mesfioui, off rue Rahba Lakdima, Medina • 0524 44 09 26 • www.riadenija.com •* Dh Dh Dh Dh

5 La Maison Arabe

More a small hotel than a riad, La Maison Arabe began life as a restaurant in the 1940s, closing in 1983 and then re-opening 16 years later as the city's first *maison d'hôtes*. It feels almost like a country mansion and retains a definite colonial air. Guests can use a lovely garden pool on the outskirts of the city in a garden setting. *Map H2 • 1 derb Assehbe, Bab Doukkala • 0524 38 70 10 • www.lamaisonarabe.com •* Dh Dh – Dh Dh Dh Dh Dh

Riad El Fenn

A riad is a house constructed around a courtyard garden.

Central courtyard at Dar Attajmil

6 Riad Kaiss

Close to Jemaa El Fna, this delightful riad once housed the harem of Sultan Moulay Yacoub. With nine rooms and suites, it boasts a *hammam*, spa, courtyard garden, restaurant and sun terraces. Services include cookery classes, tours and a personal shopper. *Map K4 • 65 derb Jedid, off rue Riad Zitoun El Kedim, Medina • 0524 44 01 41 • www.riadkaiss.com •* Dh Dh

7 Riyad Al Moussika

The Italian proprietor of this riad formerly owned by Thami El Glaoui *(see p33)* has created a traditional-style residence with six rooms on two levels, an Andalusian courtyard and a music room with a piano. The food is particularly good. *Map L4 • 17 derb Cherkaoui, off rue Douar Graoua, Medina • 0524 38 90 67 • www.riyad-al-moussika.com •* Dh Dh Dh

8 Dar Attajmil

This is a tiny riad with just four rooms overlooking a small courtyard full of banana trees. The rooms feature earthy tones and have dark-wood ceilings and *tadelakt* bathrooms *(see p36)*. The owners can arrange cookery classes and airport transfers. *Map J3 • 23 rue Laksour, Quartier Laksour, Medina • 0524 42 69 66 • www.darattajmil.com •* Dh Dh

9 Tchaikana

Reasonably priced, this riad has two suites, two big double rooms and one smaller double room. The decor in each room is beautiful and highlights the "African" in North African. The rooms are set around a large central courtyard that is used for breakfasts and candlelit dinners. *Map K2 • 25 derb El Ferrane, Quartier Azbest, Medina • 0524 38 51 50 • www.tchaikana.com •* Dh Dh

10 Riad Magi

The rooms at this English-owned riad may not be the grandest in Marrakech, but they are tastefully decorated, bright and delightful. *Map K3 • 79 derb Moulay Abdelkader, off derb Dabachi • 0524 42 66 88 • No credit cards •* Dh Dh

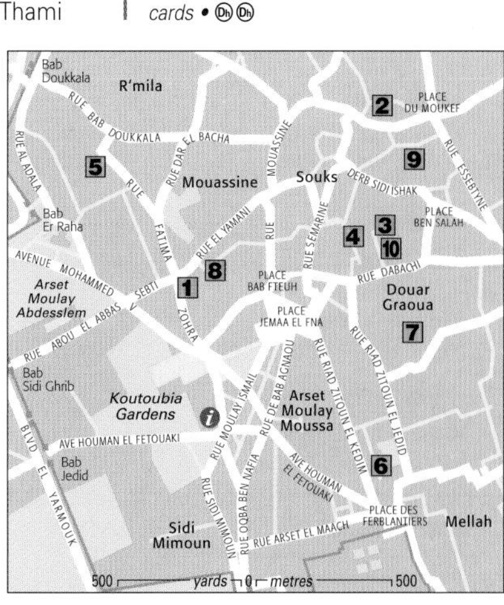

For more riads and their price categories, **see pp114–16**. *All riads accept credit cards unless otherwise stated.*

Left **The dinosaurs at Jnane El Harti** Right **Riding camels in the Palmeraie**

Top 10 Marrakech for Children

Enjoying a pony ride at Palmeraie Golf Palace

1 Jemaa El Fna

With jugglers, snake charmers, acrobats and musicians, Jemaa El Fna will definitely capture the children's imagination. However, make sure kids have adequate protection from the heat, especially during the summer months, when temperatures can top 40°C (104°F) *(see pp8–11)*.

2 Pony and camel rides

Off the main route through the Palmeraie among the palms is the Tansift Garden, which has a children's playground and the Palmier d'Or café. Ponies can be hired, and camel rides are also available nearby. *Circuit de la Palmeraie • Open 8am–11:30pm or midnight daily*

3 Calèche trips

On the north side of Place de Foucault, just off Jemaa El Fna, a ride in brightly painted horse-drawn *calèches* (carriages) might be a novel way to entertain kids. The carriages circle the medina walls or go up to the Palmeraie. Prices are listed for some tours, or you can negotiate an hourly rate (90 Dh is reasonable).

4 Swimming

The Palmeraie Golf Palace and Resort *(see p117)* allows non-guests the use of its swimming pool. It also has a children's play area and a bowling alley.

5 Horse riding

Ponies and horses can be ridden at the Palmeraie Golf Palace Hotel and Resort *(see p117)*. The Royal Club Equestre also has horses and ponies available to hire for both adults and children under ten years of age (15-minute rides are offered). *Royal Club Equestre, Route du barrage (opposite Oasiria) • 0524 38 18 49*

6 Kawkab Jeu

South of the Jnane El Harti, next to the Royal Tennis Club, this bright coffee shop serving ice cream also has indoor and outdoor play areas. Kids can have a go at playing table football, table tennis and video games. *Map C5 • 1 rue Imam Shafi, Kawkab Centre, Hivernage • 0524 43 89 29 • Open 2–10pm Tue–Fri, 9:30am–11pm Sat, Sun and holidays • www.kawkab-jeu.com*

7 Child-friendly eating

Parents of fussy eaters might be glad of Le Catanzaro, an Italian restaurant in Guéliz that makes mini pizzas for children. Alternatively, there are ubiquitous McDonald's outlets for a quick bite. *Le Catanzaro, 42 rue Tarik Ben Ziad • 0524 43 37 31 • Open noon–2:30pm, 7:30–11pm Mon–Sat; closed Aug*

8 Child-friendly accommodation

If you are travelling with kids, opt for one of the larger hotels *(see p111)*, instead of the smaller riads where noisy kids can be an issue. The Coralia Club Palmariva is child-friendly with a pool, playground and an activity centre. *Coralia Club Palmariva, Km 6, Route de Fès • 0524 32 90 36 • H3000@accor.com*

9 Oasiria

South of the city, this large waterpark features a wave pool, lagoons, a covered and heated pool, an artificial river and beach, plus many restaurants. A free shuttle bus runs every 45 minutes, from 9:30am, from Jemaa El Fna and Guéliz. *Km 4, Route du barrage • 0524 38 04 38 • Open 10am–6pm daily • Adm www.oasiria.com*

10 Jnane El Harti

This public park has a small kid's play area with two concrete grey dinosaurs for kids to climb up and slide down. There's a McDonald's opposite *(see p77)*.

Carousel at the Kawkab Jeu play area

Top 10 Other Activities

1 Cooking

Souk Cuisine organizes culinary weeks or tailor-made programmes. *www.soukcuisine.com*

2 Cycling

Bicycles can be hired from various places, including Bazaar Salah Eddine (off Rue de Bab Agnaoul) and Rue Bani Marine.

3 Golf

Play at the Palmeraie Golf Palace *(see p117)* or the Golf d'Amelkis. *Golf d'Amelkis: Km 12, Route de Ouarzazate; 0524 40 44 14*

4 Hammams & spas

A popular pastime is to strip down for a relaxing massage *(see pp40–41)*.

5 Horse riding

The Royal Club Equestre is one of several stables. *0524 38 18 49*

6 Karting

Atlas Karting on the Route de Safi also offers quad bikes. *Map C4 • 0661 23 76 87 www.atlaskarting.com*

7 Language

Learn French at the Institut Français in July. *Map B5 • Jbel Guéliz 566 • 0524 44 69 30 • www.if-maroc.org/marrakech*

8 Marathons

A marathon takes place in January. *www.marathon-marrakech.com*

9 Swimming

There are hotel pools open to non-guests at Les Jardins de la Koutoubia and Sofitel *(for both, see p111)*.

10 Tennis

The Royal Tennis Club welcomes non-members (with reservations). *Map C5 • Rue Oued El Makhazine, Guéliz • 0524 43 19 02 • www.rtc.ma*

Left **Briouettes** Right **A table set with authentic Moroccan cuisine**

TOP 10 Moroccan Cuisine

1 Couscous

A staple cuisine across North Africa, couscous comprises tiny grains of semolina that are cooked by steaming, which causes it to swell and turn light and fluffy. It is usually eaten with a spicy, harissa-flavoured broth, and served with steamed vegetables and meat.

2 Tajines

Cooked slowly at low temperatures in a clay pot with a cone-shaped lid, tajines typically combine meat with fruits. Ingredients for these dishes include any foodstuff that braises well, such as fish, beef, dried fruits, olives and vegetables.

3 Pastilla

Pastilla is a starter as well as a main dish. It is a pillow of filo pastry with a sweet and savoury stuffing – generally shredded pigeon cooked with onions. The dish is dusted with cinnamon to give it that distinctive Moroccan flavour.

4 Briouettes

Small triangles of filo pastry with a variety of fillings, the most common being minced lamb with spices and pine nuts, and feta cheese with spinach. Some kitchens in Marrakech also prepare them with shrimp, chicken and lemon. Their sweet version is prepared with groundnuts and soaked in honey.

5 Harira

A traditional Moroccan soup made with tomatoes, lentils, chickpeas, spices and lamb, it is a substantial meal by itself. Associated with special occasions, it is also served during Ramadan when it is eaten at sundown to break the fast.

A serving of Harira soup

6 Moroccan salads

Moroccan salads are served at the beginning of a meal. Orange blossom water, a signature local ingredient, is used in the preparation of some salads.

7 Moroccan pastries

The end of a meal is often marked with a serving of pastries. The popular honey cakes or *chabakia,* deep-fried and dipped in honey, are served during Ramadan. Another tasty dessert is sweet pastilla – a filo pastry covered in nuts and *crème Anglaise* (custard).

Traditional handwashing kettle

For restaurant listings where you can sample Moroccan cuisine, **see pp52–3, 65, 71, 79, 85, 93 and 99.**

A belly dancer entertains at dinner time

8 Mint tea

The ubiquitous green tea with mint is invariably served with vast quantities of sugar. The technique of pouring is almost as crucial as the drink itself; the long, curved teapot spouts allow the tea to be poured theatrically, the liquid gracefully arcing into the small glasses.

9 Set meals

In cheaper restaurants, set meals consist of a starter (soup or a salad), a main dish and a dessert (fruit or crème caramel). The more expensive restaurants serve a seemingly limitless succession of courses with more food than you could possibly eat. Indulge in it at least once for a true Marrakech experience.

10 Entertainment

Some restaurants combine dining with entertainment, such as belly dancing or performances by Gnawa musicians. Chez Ali, north of Tensift Bridge, takes kitsch to extremes, with fantasia horse riders, acrobats and snake charmers displaying their skills.

Top 10 variations on a tajine

1 Lamb, prune and roast almonds

The sliced almonds add crunch to the sticky consistency of the prunes.

2 Lamb, onions and almonds

This savoury lamb tajine is a great favourite.

3 Lamb and dates

Served at Le Tanjia *(see p65)* and widely used in French cuisine.

4 Lamb and pear

The pear all but melts to the consistency of a purée. Served at La Maison Arabe *(see p46)*.

5 Veal and green peas

The added saffron and ginger give this tajine a very special taste.

6 Beef with fennel and peas

The chefs at La Maison Arabe *(see p46)* make good use of beef in this extremely tasty tajine.

7 Kefta tajine

These are small balls of spicy minced meat that are slow-cooked in a rich tomato sauce, with an egg occasionally added.

8 Fish

Apart from Dar Moha *(see p71)*, you will find the best, freshest fish tajines in Essaouira.

9 Lamb and artichokes

Strong-flavoured lamb works beautifully with caramelised onions and artichokes.

10 Veal and quince

Those who like a mixture of sweet and sour should try this popular tajine.

Left **L'Avenue** Centre **Le Foundouk** Right **Dar Yacout**

Top 10 Restaurants

1 Le Foundouk
This stylish restaurant serves French and Moroccan cuisine. An old courtyard building has been given a modern look, complete with leather seating and a wonderful chandelier. A small bar area and a beautiful roof terrace provide the perfect spot for an apéritif while waiting for a table *(see p71)*.

2 Dar Moha
Taste Moroccan cuisine as reinterpreted by Marrakech's celebrity chef, Moha Fedal. Lunch and dinner are set menus but the food is unlike any-thing you will eat elsewhere. Musicians add to the ambience and perform by the poolside during summer *(see p71)*.

3 Al Fassia
This completely women-run Moroccan restaurant is unusual in that it offers à la carte choices rather than a set menu. The restaurant has a charming garden, but lacks the panache of its many competitors though it compensates with its terrific food *(see p79)*.

4 Chez Chegrouni
A ringside view of Jemaa El Fna makes this otherwise modest restaurant worthy of a mention. Dishes are traditional, simple and affordable, including couscous, tajines and brochettes. The evening entertainment consists of whatever is played out in the square below *(see p65)*.

5 Le Tobsil
Dine at Tobsil for a sumptuous experience. Occupying two levels of an old house around a central court, it is lit up by candlelight and has no menu; waiters deliver a seemingly endless succession of dishes – vegetarian meze, pastilla, tajines, couscous and pastries *(see p71)*.

6 Jemaa El Fna
Each evening, a part of the main square in the medina is transformed into a vast open-air eatery; crowds flock between the numerous makeshift kitchens set up to prepare food for the people assembled. It's possible to sample most Moroccan classics, from harrira and brochettes to couscous and tajines *(see pp10–11)*.

Dar Moha

For more restaurants and their price categories, **see pp65, 71, 79, 85, 93 and 99.**

Comptoir

7 Bab Restaurant

A sleek, contemporary style has made Bab one of the top spots in the city. The food is good too, with a primarily light, European menu, including dishes such as carpaccio of swordfish. *Map B5 • Cnr blvd Mansour Eddahbi and rue Mohammed El Beqal, Guéliz • 0524 43 52 50 • Open lunch and dinner daily • Credit cards accepted •* (Dh)(Dh)(Dh)(Dh)

8 Dar Yacout

As famous an attraction as the Koutoubia or the Mamounia. Much of Dar Yacout's reputation rests on its interior, a striking mix of the traditional and the bizarre, with flowering columns and candy-striped fireplaces. Sit at the mother-of-pearl-inset tables and feast on the limitless set menu *(see p71)*.

9 Comptoir

Located in a two-storey villa, this is the best venue for a night out in town. The noise levels are invariably high, with voices competing with the DJ. While the food is good, with both Moroccan and French choices, it is the atmosphere that makes Comptoir memorable, especially at weekends, when diners are entertained by belly dancers *(see p79)*.

10 L'Avenue

If it is atmosphere you're after, this is the place for you: delicious food, excellent service and a hundred flickering candles. Dishes are mainly French and Italian. L'Avenue is also a chic place to drop into for happy hour (7–9pm daily). *Map B4 • Cnr route de Targa and rue du Capitaine Arigui, Guéliz • 0524 45 89 01 • Open 10am–1am daily • Credit cards accepted •* (Dh)(Dh)(Dh)

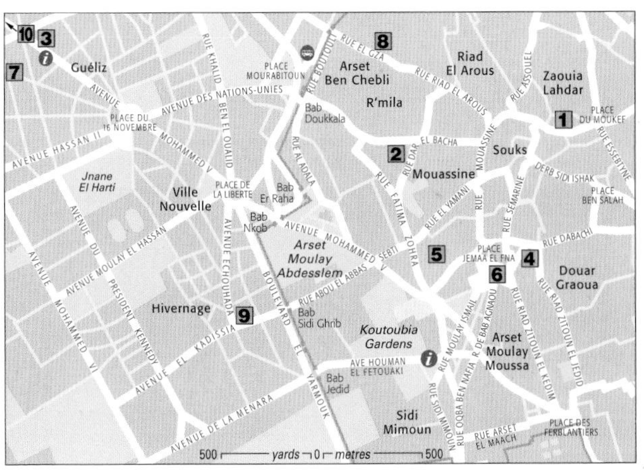

Left **Kechmara** Right **Pacha**

Top 10 Nightlife

1 Comptoir

A spacious lounge above the ground-floor restaurant *(see p79)*, with a long and alluring bar stretching along one wall, this is the place where women dress up and men turn on the charm. The atmosphere is smart and sophisticated, verging on the louche. *Map C6 • Ave Echouhada, Hivernage • 0524 43 77 02 • Open 4pm–2am daily • www.comptoirdarna.com • MC, V accepted*

2 Pacha

A 10-minute drive south of town is North Africa's largest, megadecibel, super club. A massive, purpose-built affair, it can accommodate up to 3,000 people. It also boasts a chillout lounge, two restaurants and a swimming pool with sunbathing terrace. Guest DJs are flown in from overseas every weekend. *Blvd Mohammed VI, Zone hôtelière de l'Aguedal • 0524 38 84 00 • Open noon–5am daily • www.pachamarrakech.com • MC, V accepted*

3 Café Atlas

The medina has a largely "no liquor" rule; as a result, the nightlife is mostly outside the city walls, especially around Place Abdel Moumen Ben Ali, where this café is located. Sip coffee at streetside tables or enjoy alcohol inside. *Map B5 • Ave Mohammed V, Guéliz • 0524 44 88 88 • Open 8am–10pm daily • No credit cards*

4 Kozybar

In the heart of the medina, this establishment, with a good cellar of Moroccan wines, has a ground floor with a piano, a first floor with cosy nooks and a roof terrace with amazing views. *Map K5 • 47 place des Ferblantiers • 0524 38 03 24 • Open noon–1am Tue–Sun • Credit cards accepted*

5 Kechmara

This hip café bar has a retro feel and a friendly, relaxed vibe. In addition to live music and art installations, there is beer on tap and a large food menu *(see p79)*.

Upstairs at the Comptoir lounge

So

This self-styled "night lounge" charges a hefty entrance fee (250 dh), but you get that back if you book a table for supper. Listen to live music and dance from 1am till dawn. *Map G4 • Sofitel Marrakech Palais Imperial, rue Haroun Errachid, Hivernage • 0524 42 56 00 • Open 8pm–3am daily • Credit cards accepted*

Live music at Pacha

Grand Tazi

This budget hotel's informal bar allows impecunious travellers to kick back over cheap beer. It's shabby, but one of few places to enjoy drinks in the medina. *Map J4 • Rue Almouwahidine, Bab Agnaou, Medina • 0524 44 27 87 • Open noon–11pm daily • Credit cards accepted*

Théatro

Set in a converted theatre, this hip nightclub is known for its uproarious hedonism. The former stage is now a busy dance floor. *Map C6 • Hotel Es Saadi, Ave El Kadissia, Hivernage • 0524 44 88 11 • Open 11pm–5am daily • www.theatromarrakech.com • MC, V accepted*

Nikki Beach

Lounge by the pool and swim out to the "floating bars" at this fabulously glitzy club 15 minutes from the medina. At night, it transforms into a busy nightclub with DJs playing over an amazing sound system. *Circuit de la Palmeraie • 0524 36 87 27 • Open Mar–Jan: 11:30am–midnight daily • www.nikkibeach.com • MC, V accepted*

Casino de Marrakech

Opened in 1952 with a full revue show imported from Paris, the Casino has seen the likes of Josephine Baker grace its stage. It now features 14 gaming tables and a cabaret show. *Map C6 • Rue Ibrahim El Mazini, Hivernage • 0524 44 88 11 • www.poker-marrakech.com*

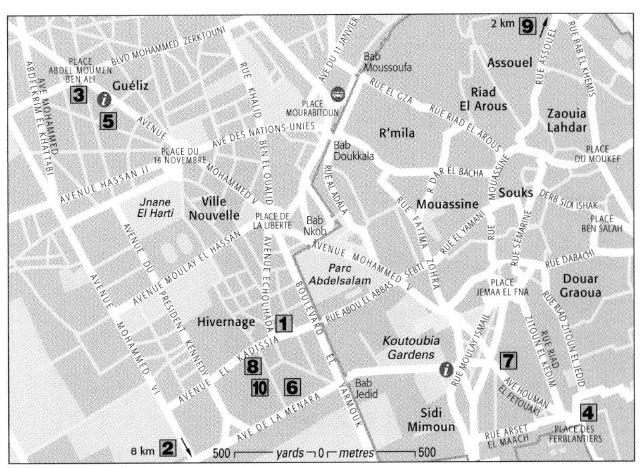

Left **Tameslohte** Right **The artificial lake, Barrage Lalla Takarkoust**

Top 10 Day Trips

1 Kasbah du Toubkal

A former tribal stronghold deep in the Atlas Mountains, this kasbah is at the foot of Jbel Toubkal. The last part of the journey is done by mule. Visitors are brought up for a Berber lunch and a hike and delivered back into town before dark. You can even stay overnight at the kasbah *(see p93)*.

2 Essaouira

This medieval walled port-city on the Atlantic coast a few hours from Marrakech, boasts rampart walks, souks, beaches, a fishing harbour and a fascinating hippy-era history *(see pp80–83)*.

3 Barrage Lalla Takarkoust

To the south of Marrakech on Route d'Amizmiz, this is an impressive artificial lake with the Atlas Mountains as a backdrop. The clear water makes it a great place to go swimming. You can also take out one of the boats for hire. Try out the fare at the many waterside restaurants, including Le Flouka, which also offers accommodation. *Map C2 • Le Flouka, BP 45 Barrage Lalla takerskoust • 0661 18 74 72 • www.leflouka.com*

4 Oukaimeden

Marrakech also serves as a base for skiing for a part of the year. Snowfall on the Atlas between February and April means business for the ski resort at Oukaimeden high above the Ourika Valley. There is a chairlift and ski equipment can be hired on site. The Bronze Age petroglyphs are an attraction in spring and summer. *Map C2*

5 Kasbah Telouet

Travellers to Ouarzazate invariably call on the imposing mountain palace of Telouet, but if your plans don't include a trip south of the Atlas, then visit the kasbah on a day trip from Marrakech. A daily bus goes to Telouet or you can hire a taxi for the day; ask your hotel to arrange it *(see p95)*.

6 Tin Mal

About two hours' drive south of Marrakech, the ancient mosque of Tin Mal makes for a stunning day out in case a full trip over the Tizi-n-Test pass is not possible.

Kasbah du Toubkal

For longer trips over the Atlas Mountains, **see pp88–99.**

If you go on Saturday, you can stop over at Asni's weekly market en route *(see p89)*.

Ourika Valley

7 Setti Fatma

You will find this small village, hidden away an hour's drive south of the city, at the head of the Ourika Valley in the foothills of the Atlas Mountains. It's the starting point for a 15-minute stroll up to a fine waterfall and pool – and then a strenuous hike up a steep valley to six more falls. *Map C2*

8 Country markets

Several small villages in the vicinity of Marrakech host weekly markets. Villagers from surrounding regions flock to them to buy and sell produce, cheap clothing and assorted bric-a-brac. Donkeys and mules are the dominant means of transport. Cattle auctions are also common, as are makeshift salons of travelling barbers and dentists. Ask your hotel for details on where and when to find them.

9 Tameslohte

A 20-minute drive out of Marrakech on the Route d'Amizmiz, Tameslohte is a roadside village famed for its busy potters' cooperative. There's also an ancient mule-driven olive oil press, weavers' workshops and a crumbling kasbah. Start your trip by paying a visit to the Association Tameslohte, an information office on the main square, Place Sour Souika, next to the main mosque. If this office is shut, one of the locals will be able to tell you where to find the potters. *Map C1*

10 Cascades d'Ouzoud

Two hours northeast on Route de Fès, these are the most beautiful waterfalls in Morocco. Trek through wooded groves (*ouzoud* is Berber for olives) to reach the gorges of Oued El Abid. There's a lovely riad at the top of the Cascades if you fancy spending the night. *Map D1 • Riad Cascades d'Ouzoud • 0523 42 91 73 • www.ouzoud.com*

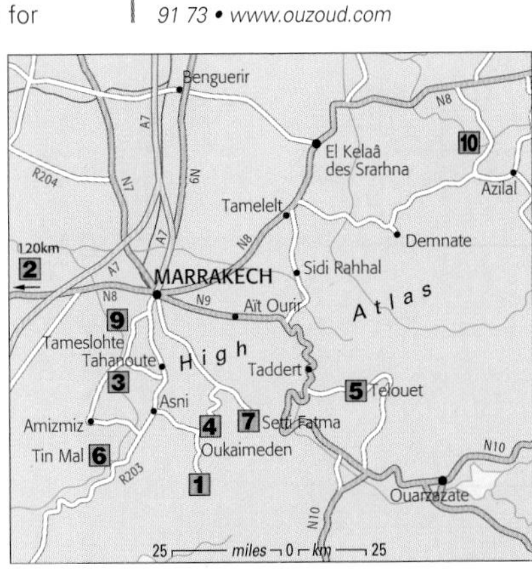

Cheap buses head over the mountains, or you could hire a car or your own driver in the form of a grand taxi. For details, **see p104.**

AROUND TOWN

Jemaa El Fna and the Kasbah 60–65

The Souks 66–71

The New City 74–79

Essaouira 80–85

Tizi-n-Test Pass 88–93

Tizi-n-Tichka Pass 94–99

Left **Maison Tiskiwine** Right **Bahia Palace**

Jemaa El Fna and the Kasbah

THE SPIRITUAL AND HISTORICAL HEART OF MARRAKECH, *the Jemaa El Fna (pronounced as a rushed "j'maf na") was laid out as a parade ground by the city's founders* (see pp8–11)*. After the new rulers of Marrakech constructed a walled royal domain to the south – known as the kasbah – the open ground passed into the public domain. Sultans have come and gone and royal palaces have risen and fallen, but the Jemaa El Fna remains eternally vital. Used earlier to display the heads of executed criminals, it is still home to some extraordinary sights, like snake charmers and tooth pullers. By night, it transforms into a busy eating area.*

Lane near Rue de Bab Agnaou

TOP 10 Sights

1. Koutoubia Mosque
2. Rue de Bab Agnaou
3. Saadian Tombs
4. Badii Palace
5. Rue Riad Zitoun El Kedim
6. Mellah
7. Bahia Palace
8. Rue Riad Zitoun El Jedid
9. Dar Si Said Museum
10. Maison Tiskiwine

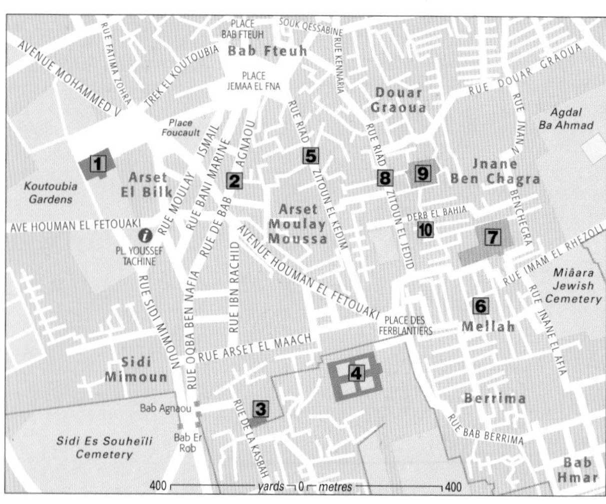

Preceding pages **Bahia Palace**

Koutoubia Mosque

1 Koutoubia Mosque

The Koutoubia Mosque is easily identified by its magnificent minaret or tower. And what a beautiful structure it is; at a towering height of 77 metres (252 ft), its rose pink colour makes for an eye-catching contrast, silhouetted against the cobalt blue sky by daylight and in the fiery orange twilight of the evenings *(see pp12–13)*. Only Muslims are permitted inside the mosque.

2 Rue de Bab Agnaou

Running south off Jemaa El Fna, this is the medina's pedestrianised "modern" main street. Though not a particularly picturesque street, it is a very serviceable one with postcard sellers, cash-dispensing ATMs, telephone offices, pharmacies and Internet cafés. Its narrow side alleys are home to hotels that are easy on the wallet. While in the city, you will definitely find yourself making a trip here to make use of its many facilities. *Map J4*

3 Saadian Tombs

The historic Saadian tombs are located down a narrow passageway that runs beside the Kasbah Mosque, which itself is just inside the beautiful and equally historic Bab Agnaou *(see p18)*. The small garden site is the final resting place for some 66 royals who belonged to the Saadian dynasty, whose reign marked a golden era in the history of the city *(see pp20–21)*.

4 Badii Palace

It is difficult to reconcile these ruins with a palace once reputed to be among the world's finest. An expanse of dusty ground within half-eroded walls, it retains some of its old elements, including sunken gardens and a dazzling piece of Moorish craftsmanship *(see pp24–5)*.

5 Rue Riad Zitoun El Kedim

This "Street of the Old Olive Garden" connects Jemaa El Fna with the palace quarter. At its north end a narrow lane squeezed between the blank walls of mosques and townhouses, it widens southwards, where it's lined with workshops. *Map K4*

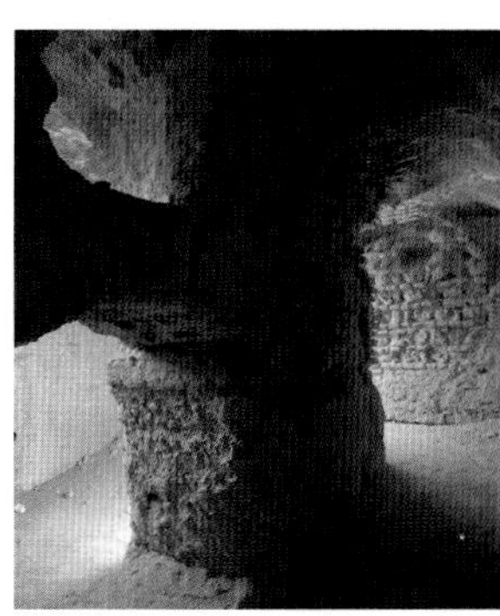
Underground passage at the Badii Palace

The King and his Palaces

Throughout Moroccan history, the royal court has shifted base between Fès, Meknès, Rabat and Marrakech. The Almohads furnished Marrakech with its first royal palace south of Jemaa El Fna in the 12th century, and it's been there ever since. The present King Mohammed VI had a smaller palace built for his personal use, outside the Bab Agnaou.

6 Mellah

The old Jewish quarter lies immediately east of the kasbah. You can enter via the Souk El Bab Salaam, a busy, covered market street across from a rose-planted square. This street leads to Place Souweka and just to the north you'll find one of the city's last working synagogues. Most of the Jewish population of Marrakech left for Israel after the Second World War, in the 1950s and 1960s, but the number of graves in the nearby Miâara Jewish cemetery is testament to how many there once were.

Map L5

7 Bahia Palace

Built in the 1890s by a powerful grand vizier (high official), the Bahia ("Brilliant") is a minor palace complex approached by a long garden driveway. Inside, arrows direct visitors through a succession of courtyards and private rooms that were used by the vizier and his four wives. All the rooms are lavishly decorated with *zellij* tiling *(see p36)*, sculpted stucco and carved cedarwood. The ruling sultan, Abdel Aziz, was so jealous of the riches of the Bahia that on the vizier's death he had the palace stripped and looted.

Map K5 • Rue Riad Zitoun El Jedid • 0524 38 91 79 • Open 8:45–11:45am, 2:45–5:45pm Sat–Thu, 8:45–11:30am, 3–5:45pm Fri • Adm

8 Rue Riad Zitoun El Jedid

A long arcing alley which translates as the "Street of the New Olive Garden", this is another main route through the southern part of the medina. It connects several major sights with Jemaa El Fna, including the Bahia Palace and Dar Si Said Museum. You will also come across the small *derb* (area) that leads to Riad Tamsna, a restaurant, gallery and boutique, housed in a beautiful old courtyard building that has upper galleries and a roof terrace.

Map K4 • Riad Tamsna: 23 derb Zanka Daika • 0524 38 52 72 • Open noon–midnight daily

Souk El Bab Salaam

9 Dar Si Said Museum

Built by the brother of Ba Ahmed, builder of the Bahia Palace, this is an altogether more modest dwelling. However, what it sacrifices in scale, it makes up for in its impressive detailing – the house has some beautiful

Dar Si Said Museum

painted ceilings. It also serves as a museum for decorative arts; the exhibits on display include fine examples of carved wooden panels and painted Berber doors. The museum also includes some interestingly designed jewellery, carpets and metalwork. *Map K4 • Rue Riad Zitoun El Jedid • 0524 44 24 64 • Open 9am–noon, 3–6:30pm Wed–Mon • Adm*

10 Maison Tiskiwine

Located en route to the Dar Si Said Museum, this is a private house belonging to the Dutch anthropologist Bert Flint. An avid documenter of tribal arts and crafts, particularly carpets, Flint had amassed a fascinating and vast collection. Presented in his home for public viewing, the exhibition has been organized geographically as a journey that traces the old desert trade routes from Marrakech to Timbuktu. Unfortunately, you'll find the labelling of the exhibits in French only. *Map K4 • 8 derb El Bahia, off rue Riad Zitoun El Jedid • 0524 38 91 92 • Open 9am–12:30pm, 3–6pm daily • Adm*

To the palaces

Morning

Start on **Jemaa El Fna** *(see pp8–11)*. On the south side is an arch that leads through **Rue Riad Zitoun El Kedim** *(see p61)*. This area is mainly inhabited by locals and there's an absence of souvenir and trinket vendors. At the southern end of the street, several places sell items fashioned out of old car tyres, from the purely practical (buckets) to the quirky (stylish mirror frames). Over the main road, is the **Marché Couvert** *(see p64)*, a fruit, vegetable and meat market, worth a quick look. Then just southeast is the **Place des Ferblantiers** *(see p64)*, a paved plaza surrounded by metal-workers, with a gate that leads through to the haunting **Badii Palace** *(see p61)*. After visiting the ruins, grab a cheap snack on the northwest corner of Place des Ferblantiers.

Afternoon

Wander through the **Souk El Bab Salaam** *(see p64)* before heading back north up the **Rue Riad Zitoun El Jedid**. At the end of the street, on the right is the gateway to the **Bahia Palace**, but anyone pushed for time should turn right and take the first left to the excellent **Dar Si Said Museum**. Along Rue Riad Zitoun El Jedid to the left is **Riad Tamsna**, worth dropping in to shop and have a cup of tea. Further north is a good little boutique, **Jamade** *(see p64)*. Pass by the **Cinéma Eden**, one of the city's few open-air picture houses, and bear left to re-emerge onto Jemaa El Fna.

Left **Souk El Bab Salaam** Centre **1920s postcard in Aya's shop** Right **Akkal pottery at Jamade**

TOP 10 Places to Shop

1 Centre Artisanal

This vast government-run storehouse is just a few minutes' walk from the Saadian Tombs. You'll find an array of traditional Moroccan handicrafts, from carpets to pottery. The prices are fixed, so no haggling *(see p21)*.

2 Dinanderie

Displaying the work of Moulay Youssef, a famous Moroccan metalworker, this charming atelier is hidden away in an alley west of the rose garden across the Place des Ferblantiers. *Map K5 • 6–46 Fondouk My Mamoun • 0524 38 49 09*

3 Marché Couvert

Commonly called the Mellah Market, this indoor market sells local produce including dried fruit, nuts, meat and fish. *Map K5 • Ave Houman El Fetouaki • Closed Fri*

4 Souk El Bab Salaam

Follow the aromas, wafting from the edge of the old Jewish quarter, to this small market selling herbs and spices. *Map K5*

5 Place des Ferblantiers

As an alternative to the souks, this is the place to go to for the unique brass and iron lanterns that come in all shapes and sizes, including some inset with coloured glass. *Map K5*

6 Rue Riad Zitoun El Jedid

This street is lined with small boutiques offering an alternative to the souks *(see p62)*.

7 Jamade

A quirky boutique offering stylish handicrafts, ceramics and jewellery, including products made by rural women. Fixed prices, so no haggling! *Map K4 • 1 place Douar Graoua, rue Riad Zitoun El Jedid • 0524 42 90 42*

8 Le Cadeau Berbère

Established in 1930, this family-run textile specialist boasts an international clientele of interior designers, hoteliers and collectors. *Map J3 • 51 Jemaa El Fna • 0524 44 29 07*

9 Aya's

It may be hard to find (a door away from Le Tanjia), but worth seeking out for exotic clothing and jewellery, as well as curiosities such as saucy "ethnic" postcards from the 1920s. *Map K5 • 11 bis, Derb Jedid, Bab Mellah • 05 24 38 34 28 • www.ayasmarrakech.com*

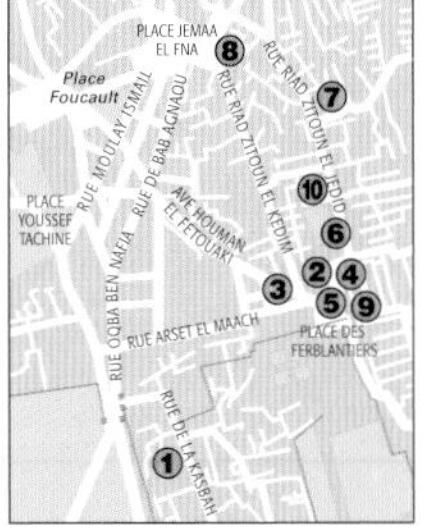

10 Cordonnerie Errafia

A small shoemaker who specializes in stylish loafers fashioned from raffia for men, and more decorative ones for women. *Map K4 • Rue Riad Zitoun El Jedid • 0662 77 83 47*

Pizzeria Venezia

Price Categories

For a full meal for one with half a bottle of wine (or equivalent meal), plus taxes and extra charges.

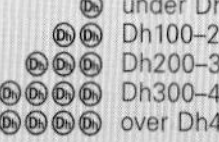

Dh	under Dh100
Dh Dh	Dh100–200
Dh Dh Dh	Dh200–300
Dh Dh Dh Dh	Dh300–400
Dh Dh Dh Dh Dh	over Dh400

Top 10 Places to Eat

1 Les Prémises

The upstairs terrace offers views over the main square. On the menu are Moroccan favourites and pizza. *Map J3 • Jemaa El Fna • 0524 39 19 70 • Open 8am–11pm daily • No credit cards • Dh Dh*

2 Le Marrakchi

This restaurant has an à la carte menu, music and belly dancing. *Map K3 • 52 rue des Banques • 0524 44 33 77 • Open 11:30am–3pm, 7:30pm–midnight daily • www.lemarrakchi.com • MC, V accepted • Dh Dh Dh*

3 Terrasses de l'Alhambra

Enjoy the pizzas and pastas on this eatery's first-floor terrace. *Map K3 • Jemaa El Fna • Open 8am–11pm daily • No credit cards • Dh Dh*

4 Narwarma

Set in a mansion, the Thai food matches the resplendent surroundings. *Map J4 • 30 rue de la Koutoubia • 0524 44 08 44 • Open 7pm–1am daily • MC, V accepted • Dh Dh*

5 Kozybar

Eat out on the lovely terrace overlooking the kasbah walls. *Map K5 • 47 place des Ferblantiers • 0524 38 03 24 • Open noon–1am Tue–Sun • MC, V accepted • Dh Dh Dh*

6 Pâtisserie des Princes

A local version of a French pastry parlour, this place also offers ice creams, juices, tea and coffee. *Map J4 • 32 rue de Bab Agnaou • 0524 44 30 33 • Open 5am–11pm daily*

7 Chez Chegrouni

Dine on the roof terrace while enjoying views of the stalls, snake charmers and jugglers. Tasty, well-priced local dishes. *Map K3 • Jemaa El Fna • 0665 47 46 15 • Open 6am–11pm daily • No credit cards • Dh*

8 Le Tanjia

A three-floored temple of fine dining and entertainment, with an excellent Moroccan menu and belly dancers at night. *Map K5 • 14 derb Jedid, Hay Essalam, Mellah • 0524 38 38 36 • Open noon–3:30pm, 7:30pm–1am daily • Credit cards accepted • Dh Dh Dh*

9 Jemaa El Fna

For the ultimate dining experience, try one of the stalls in the square. Play safe with brochettes (kebabs) or experiment with snail soup or smoked goat's head *(see pp10–11)*.

10 Pizzeria Venezia

The pizzas are good here, but for the best views of the Koutoubia you should head for the terrace of the attached Ground Zero Café (previously known as Venezia Ice). *Map J4 • 279 ave Mohammed V • 0524 44 00 81 • Open noon–3pm, 6–11pm daily • MC, V accepted • Dh Dh*

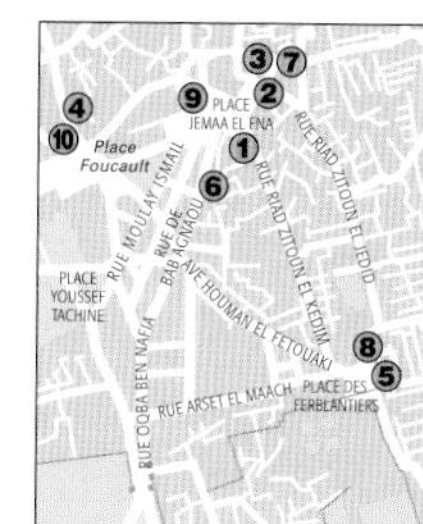

Left **Medersa Ben Youssef** Right **Detail of Koubba El Badiyin interiors**

The Souks

NORTH OF JEMAA EL FNA *is one vast area of tightly squeezed commerce with dozens of narrow alleyways, all lined with shops the size of cupboards selling cloth, leather, metalwork, brass lanterns, carpets and jewellery. Each area is dedicated to a single item, so a street might be packed with nothing but sellers of canary-yellow leather slippers and another with vendors of glazed pottery. Don't fall for the sellers' flattering cry, "Hey my friend, for you I give special price": it always pays to haggle. Irrespective of whether you are buying or not, it is an entrancing experience.*

Shoppers browsing through wares in the busy souk area

TOP 10 Sights

1. Mouassine Fountain
2. Dar Cherifa
3. Fondouks
4. Souk des Teinturiers
5. The Kissaria
6. Musée de Marrakech
7. Medersa Ben Youssef
8. Koubba El Badiyin
9. The Tanneries
10. Dar El Bacha

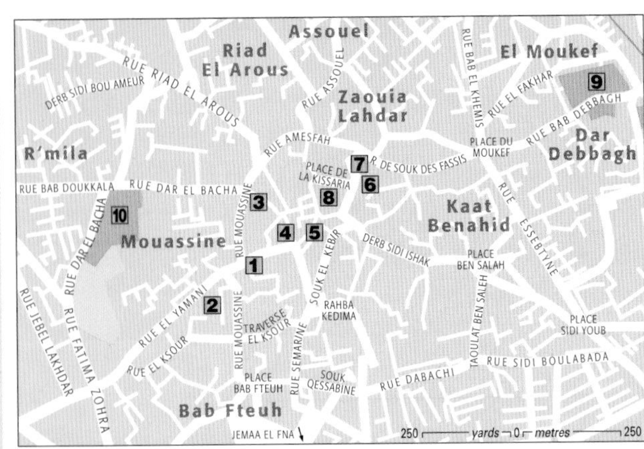

1 Mouassine Fountain

There are two main routes into the souks: Rue Mouassine and Rue Semarine. The former runs past the Mouassine Mosque, after which the neighbourhood is named. A right turn at the mosque leads to a small plaza that holds a fountain with four bays, three for animals and one for humans. An arched gateway next to the fountain leads to the Souk des Teinturiers *(see below)*. *Map J2*

2 Dar Cherifa

This beautifully renovated town house can be located by following the signs at the head of the alley opposite the side of the Mouassine Mosque. Boasting exquisite woodwork and carved plasterwork, some of the interiors date back to the 16th century. The house operates as a cultural centre, hosting regular shows by local artists. There's also a small library and tea and coffee served. *Map J2 • 8 derb Charfa Lakbir, Mouassine • 0524 39 16 09 • Open 9am–7pm daily • www.marrakech-riads.net*

3 Fondouks

To the north of the Mouassine Mosque, past Café Arabe *(see p71)*, is an excellent example of a *fondouk* or old merchants' hostel. Currently the rooms on the ground floor are used as workshops and the ones upstairs are mainly used for storage purposes. This particular fondouk has had a brush with moviedom, when it featured in the film *Hideous Kinky* as the hotel where actress Kate Winslet and her daughters are shown to be lodged. *Map J2 • 192 rue Mouassine*

Mouassine Fountain

4 Souk des Teinturiers

One of the most alluring places in Marrakech, the Dyers' Souk is a tangle of narrow alleyways east of the Mouassine Mosque. It becomes a riot of colours during the days, when hanks of just-dyed wools are hung out to dry above certain alleys. The dyers themselves are very easy to identify; they are the men with red, purple and blue colours up to their elbows *(see p14)*.

Fondouk El Mizane

For more on the souks, **see pp14–15.**

5 The Kissaria

The deepest part of the souks, the *kissaria* is a tight grouping of narrow, parallel alleys that run, much like the rungs of a ladder, between the Souk El Kebir and Souk des Babouches. Most of the shops are no bigger than cupboards and the passageway between them scarcely wide enough for two people to pass. A visit here is like stepping into the past, until a shopkeeper enquires whether you'd like to pay by cash or card. *Map K2*

6 Musée de Marrakech

This splendid, finely restored 19th-century palace houses the Fondation Omar Benjelloun, ethnological and archaeological material and a wide-ranging collection of ancient and contemporary artwork. The former *hammam* makes an unusual exhibition space. Books, postcards, tea, coffee and pastries are also sold here. *Map K2 • Place Ben Youssef • 0524 44 18 93 • Open 9am–6pm daily (except religious holidays) • Adm • www.musee.ma*

The Tanneries

The Seven Saints

Marrakech has seven patron saints, all of whom are believed to be sleeping and will one day rise again. The medina is dotted with the green-roofed shrines of the saints, all off limits to non-Muslims, though it is possible to walk through the outer precincts of the Shrine of Sidi Bel Abbes. Once a year, pilgrims flood into the city to visit a shrine a day.

7 Medersa Ben Youssef

North of the Musée de Marrakech, the Medersa is an even more stunning building. A 16th-century theological college, it has tiny, windowless cells for several hundred students and a still functioning bathroom. The real glory, however, is the central courtyard, which combines polychromic tiling, decorative plasterwork and carved-wood panelling to sublime effect *(see pp22–3)*.

8 Koubba El Badiyin

The dusty open plaza across the Musée de Marrakech is named after the Ben Youssef Mosque, lying beyond a wall on the north side. Although non-Muslims are forbidden to enter the mosque, all visitors are allowed into the Koubba El Badiyin, a small domed structure that sits alone in its own garden. This is the only surviving structure from the Almoravids era, the founders of Marrakech. The underside of the dome carries a beautiful eight-pointed star motif. *Map K2 • Place Ben Youssef • 0524 44 18 93 • Open Apr–Sep 9am–6pm daily; Oct–Mar 9am–6pm daily (except religious holidays) • Adm • www.musee.ma*

9 The Tanneries

A strong stomach is required to visit this particular quarter of the medina. This is where animal

A "three monuments" pass for 60 Dh gives admission to Musée de Marrakech, Medersa Ben Youssef and the Koubba El Badiyin.

Souk des Teinturiers

hides are turned into leather. The work is done by hand and involves the hides being soaked in open vats, which look like a paintbox of watercolours from a distance, but up close smell so foul that the guides hand out sprigs of mint to hold under your nose. The tanneries are scheduled to move elsewhere due to the pollution caused. If you venture this far, pay a visit to the nearby Bab Debbagh *(see p19)*. *Map L1*

10 Dar El Bacha

This is the former residence of Thami El Glaoui *(see pp33, 96)*, the much-feared and little-loved ruler of Marrakech and southern Morocco during the first half of the 20th century. Here Glaoui entertained guests such as Winston Churchill and kept his extensive harem. But beyond the colourful history associated with the place, the complex veers towards the tawdry. Parts of the palace, currently closed to visitors, are set to house the collection of American philanthropist Patti Birch. *Map J2 • Rue Dar El Bacha • Open 9am–2pm Mon–Fri • Adm*

Hidden Marrakech

Morning

Wrong turns and too many distractions make it impossible to plan a walk through the souks, which you should explore by yourself. On another day, head up Rue Mouassine. At the first crossroads, look left: a lantern dangles above the door of the **Kssour Agafay** *(see p45)*, the city's exclusive "members' club" (ask and you might be allowed to look around). Continue north and take the next left, then the first right to the gem that is **Dar Cherifa** *(see p67)*. Return to Rue Mouassine and turn left at the T-junction. Take the first right through a low archway; follow the alley left and then right to No. 22 and ring the bell for **Ministerio del Gusto**, a studio and gallery (9am–noon, 4–7pm). Back on the main street, take a left to the **Mouassine Fountain** *(see p67)* and then start heading northward. Stop at the **Café Arabe** *(see p71)* for lunch.

Afternoon

Ahead of the café is the **fondouk** made famous in *Hideous Kinky (see p67)*. The Shrine of Sidi Abdel Aziz is barred to non-Muslims, so take a left. On Rue Dar El Bacha, you will find many antique emporiums and the **Dar El Bacha**. Along Rue Bab Doukkala, stop at the shopping emporium, **Mustapha Blaoui** *(see p70)*. Walk west past the **Bab Doukkala Mosque**, through a street market to the **Bab Doukkala gate** *(see p19)* and the exit from the medina; this place is packed with taxis – it is 10 Dh to Jemaa El Fna.

Left **La Maison du Kaftan Marocain** Centre **Kif Kif** Right **Mustapha Blaoui**

Top 10 Places to Shop

1 Mustapha Blaoui

Monsieur Blaoui's twinkling warehouse of Moroccan goods has everything from candle-holders to wardrobes. *Map H2 • 142 rue Bab Doukkala • 0524 38 52 40*

2 Ensemble Artisanal

A government store of Moroccan handicrafts. Though not as much fun as the souks, it's less stressful. *Map H3 • Ave Mohammed V • 0524 38 66 74*

3 Atelier Moro

Above the gate beside the Mouassine fountain, this shop sells exquisite own-label clothing and accessories, plus jewellery by local designers. *Map J2 • 114 place de Mouassine • 0524 39 16 78*

4 Kif Kif

This shop sells ethno-chic gifts, including a range of wares made by women's cooperatives. Kif Kif also distributes old clothes and supports local charities. *Map J3 • 8 rue des Ksours • 06 61 08 20 41*

5 La Maison du Kaftan Marocain

Dress up like a local in the flowing robes sold here. Styles range from sedate browns to the most outrageously embroidered items in silk. *Map J2 • 65 rue Sidi El Yamani, Mouassine • 0524 44 10 51*

6 Souk Kimakhine

The instrument bazaar offers *taras* (tambourines), *gnawas* (guitars) and *tarijas* (drums) made by local craftsmen, who may play them before you buy. *Map K2*

7 Miloud El Jouli

Deep in the *kissaria*, this hard-to-find boutique attracts fans from Europe and America with its own-brand clothing and clever designer-label copies. *Map K2 • 6–8 Souk Smat El Marga • 0524 42 67 16*

8 Bazaar du Sud

Of the countless carpet shops in the souk, this has possibly the largest selection, backed up by a professional sales service. *Map K2 • 117 Souk des Tapis • 0524 44 30 04*

9 L'Art du Bain

This store deals in hand-made soaps, from the traditional Moroccan *savon noir* to natural soaps infused with rose or musk. *Map K3 • 13 Souk el Lbadine • 068 44 59 42 • www.lartdubain.com*

10 Beldi

This tiny boutique at the entrance to the souks show-cases the work of brothers Toufik and Abdelhafid. They adapt Moroccan clothing for Western tastes to stunning effect. *Map J3 • 9–11 rue Laksour • 0524 44 10 76*

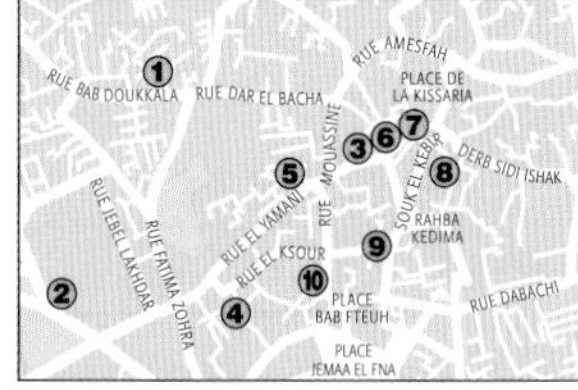

Dar Moha

Price Categories

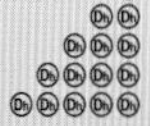

For a full meal for one with half a bottle of wine (or equivalent meal), plus taxes and extra charges.		
	Dh	under Dh100
	DhDh	Dh100–200
	DhDhDh	Dh200–300
	DhDhDhDh	Dh300–400
	DhDhDhDhDh	over Dh400

Top 10 Places to Eat

1 Le Pavillon
This long-standing French restaurant with beautiful interiors is set around a tree-shaded courtyard. *Map H2 • 47 derb Zaouia • 0524 38 70 40 • Open 7:30pm–midnight Mon, Wed–Sun • Cards accepted • DhDhDhDh*

2 La Maison Arabe
Colonial-style restaurant with a 1940s atmosphere. Tea and pastries from 10am, or enjoy dinner from 7:30pm. *Map H2 • No 1 rue Assehbe • 0524 38 70 10 • Open daily • Cards accepted • DhDhDhDhDh*

3 Café Arabe
Lounge on the pillow-strewn roof terrace. The food is Italian and Moroccan. *Map J2 • 184 rue Mouassine • 0524 42 97 28*

4 Le Foundouk
Wonderfully stylish restaurant with a French-Moroccan menu. *Map K2 • 55 rue du Souk des Fassis • 0524 37 81 90 • Open noon–4pm, 7pm–midnight Tue–Sun • MC, V accepted • DhDhDhDh*

5 Stylia
Dine at a petal-strewn table at this top restaurant housed in a 16th-century palace. *Map J3 • 34 rue Ksour • 0524 44 35 87 • Open for dinner daily • Cards accepted • DhDhDhDhDh*

6 Dar Moha
Sit by the pool and enjoy the exceptional food. *Map H2 • 81 rue Dar El Bacha • 0524 38 64 00/38 62 64 • Open 12:30–2:30pm, 7:30–10:30pm Tue–Sun • AmEx, MC, V accepted • DhDhDhDh*

7 Dar Yacout
Dine here for a typical Marrakech experience, more for the entertainment and decor than the food. *Map H1 • 79 rue Ahmed Soussi, Arset Ihiri • 0524 38 29 29 • Open 8pm–1am Tue–Sun • MC, V accepted • DhDhDhDhDh*

8 Café des Epices
Calm and charming, this café is a welcome break from the packed souk. Enjoy a mint tea on the roof terrace. *Map K3 • 75 Rahba Lakdima • 0524 39 17 70 • Open daily • No credit cards • Dh*

9 Le Tobsil
Beautiful decor, charming atmosphere, intimate and great food – it's just a pity that it's a set menu. *Map J3 • 22 derb Moulay Abdellah Ben Hessain, Bab Ksour • 0524 44 40 52 • Open 7:30–11pm Mon, Wed–Sun • MC, V accepted • DhDhDhDhDh*

10 Riad des Mers
This French seafood restaurant is supplied with a fresh catch each day – deliveries are direct from the Atlantic coast. *Map D4 • 411 derb Sidi Messaoud, Bab Yacout • 0524 37 53 04 • Open noon–3pm, 8pm–midnight daily • DhDhDh*

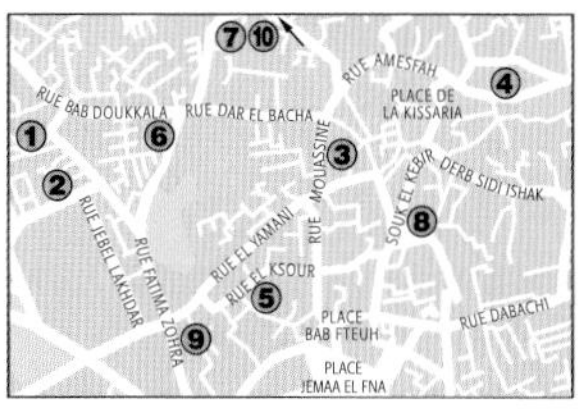

Left **The busy Avenue Mohammed V** Right **A pavement café**

The New City

IT WAS ONLY WITH THE ARRIVAL *of the French in the early 20th century that Marrakech broke out of the walls of the medina. The new colonial rulers preferred to live away from the native quarters and so built their own* nouvelle ville *of broad avenues, villas and parks. Over time, Moroccans aspiring for a better lifestyle moved out into this new town, lured by serviceable plumbing, electricity and cars. Now known as Guéliz – from the name of the hill that rises above it – the New City has plenty for tourists looking to explore the city's modern facet. The streets are lined with numerous fine restaurants, some good shopping options and a throbbing nightlife culture.*

The magnificent façade of the Théâtre Royal

Top 10 Sights

1. Avenue Mohammed V
2. Mauresque architecture
3. Hotel La Renaissance
4. Église des Saints-Martyrs de Marrakech
5. Jnane El Harti
6. Théâtre Royal
7. European cemetery
8. Spanish Quarter
9. Majorelle Gardens
10. Hivernage

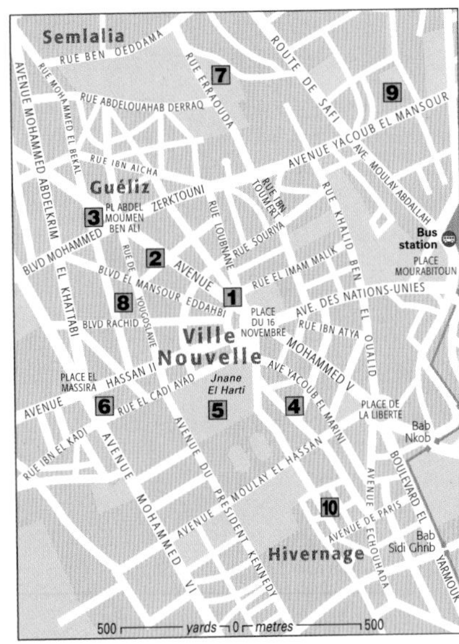

Preceding pages **Souk Attarine**

Shops along Avenue Mohammed V

1 Avenue Mohammed V

The wide avenue named after Morocco's first king is the spine of Marrakech. It connects the old and new cities, running from the Koutoubia to Jbel Guéliz (Mount Guéliz), a grandly named rocky outcrop northwest of the town. Along the way are three major traffic circles: Place de la Liberté with its modern fountain; Place du 16 Novembre where the main post office is located; and the heart of the New City, Place Abdel Moumen Ben Ali. *Map C5*

2 Mauresque architecture

The French brought with them European architectural styles, which mixed with local Moorish influences to create a new style, dubbed "Mauresque". Avenue Mohammed V is dotted with structures that were built within this particular style, especially where it intersects with Rue de la Liberté; here several buildings have clean Modernist lines but also have pavement arcades to shade pedestrians from the blazing North African sun.

3 Hotel La Renaissance

Built in 1952, La Renaissance was the first hotel in the modern district of Guéliz, and has since become an iconic building in Marrakech. The rooftop terrace is the highest in the city and gives a breathtaking panorama of the whole of the Guéliz area. The perfect spot to sample cocktails and take in the splendour of the Koutoubia *(see p61)* and the snowy peaks of the Atlas Mountains. *Map C5 • 89 Angle Bld Zerktouni et Mohamed V Gueliz • 0524 33 77 77 • www.renaissance-hotel-marrakech.com*

4 Église des Saints-Martyrs de Marrakech

Built in 1926, this Catholic church stands as a tribute to six 13th-century Franciscan friars who were beheaded by the sultan as a punishment for preaching Christianity in Morocco. Its spartan interior is enlivened by colourful panels of stained glass. The church's bell tower is now almost entirely overshadowed by the minaret of an adjacent mosque. Protestant services are conducted in the library on Sunday mornings at 10:30am. *Map C5 • Rue El Imam Ali, Guéliz • 0524 43 05 85 • Services 6:30pm Mon–Sat, 10am Sun*

Église des Saints-Martyrs de Marrakech

For more on Moroccan architecture and design styles, **see pp36–9.**

Hippyville

Before the medina's hotel boom, those who couldn't afford the Mamounia, or considered it too establishment, stayed in Guéliz. The Es Saadi in Hivernage was popular with the Rolling Stones, while Beat writer William Burroughs shacked up at Hotel Toulousain *(see p112)*. The big hippy hang-out at the time was the Renaissance.

5 Jnane El Harti

A small and very pretty park just off Place du 16 Novembre, Jnane El Harti was originally laid out by the French as a formal garden and zoo. In a 1939 essay titled "Marrakech", George Orwell *(see p34)* writes of feeding gazelles here. Numerous notices provide information about the various species of plants growing in the many flowerbeds. The plaza fronting the park gates is often used for events. *Map C5*

Modernist Guéliz architecture

6 Théâtre Royal

This striking piece of architecture by leading local light,

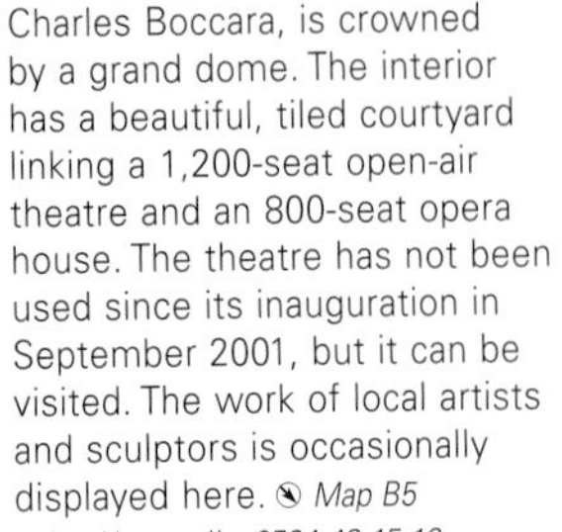

Charles Boccara, is crowned by a grand dome. The interior has a beautiful, tiled courtyard linking a 1,200-seat open-air theatre and an 800-seat opera house. The theatre has not been used since its inauguration in September 2001, but it can be visited. The work of local artists and sculptors is occasionally displayed here. *Map B5*

• Ave Hassan II • 0524 43 15 16

• Open 8:30am–7pm daily

7 European cemetery

North of Boulevard Mohammed Zerktouni is a walled graveyard dating back to the 1920s. It is the burial ground of many of the original inhabitants of Guéliz. A dozen English Protestant missionaries also rest here. Most notable is the tomb of Kate Hosali, who founded SPANA, a charity for working animals of the world, in 1923 after being appalled by the maltreatment of Morocco's beasts of burden. *Map C4 • Rue Erraouda • Open Apr–Sep 7am–7pm; Oct–Mar 8am–6pm*

Jnane El Harti

8 Spanish Quarter

Running west off Rue de Yougoslavie is a narrow street lined with single-storey houses of a unique design, much like terraced cottages. This shady lane, planted with mulberry trees, constitutes the city's old Spanish quarter, a testament to Marrakech's once considerable Hispanic

For more art and culture venues in Marrakech, **see pp44–5.**

Majorelle Gardens

population. The small houses, formerly brightly coloured, are now a uniform Marrakech pink. *Map B5*

9 Majorelle Gardens

A 10-minute walk east of Place Abdel Moumen Ben Ali, these gardens are the absolute must-see sight in the New City. Created in the 1920s and 1930s by the French painter Jacques Majorelle, the artist's former studio now houses an Islamic Art Museum. The gardens were owned by French couturier Yves Saint-Laurent until his death in 2008 and are open to the public *(see pp26–7)*.

10 Hivernage

South of Guéliz and immediately west of the medina walls, Hivernage is a small neighbourhood of quiet streets that are shaded by trees. Its mix of villas and a handful of five-star hotels ensures a tranquil atmosphere with light pedestrian traffic. There are one or two good restaurants in the area, including the city's favourite nightspot, Comptoir *(see p54)*. *Map C6*

Old city to New

Morning

Start next to the Koutoubia Mosque and head up Avenue Mohammed V. After a few minutes you will come to **Ensemble Artisanal** *(see p70)* on the right, a government-run handicraft store. Over the road is **Arset Moulay Abdesslem** *(see p43)*, known as "Cyber Park" after its Internet centre. Exit the medina from Mohammed V through the Bab Nkob, plunging into the large traffic island, Place de la Liberté. A second left after the traffic junction, followed by the first right, will lead you to historic **Église des Saints-Martyrs de Marrakech** *(see p75)*. Continue north up Avenue Yacoub Marini to reach **Jnane El Harti** park. Lunch at the **Grand Café de la Poste** *(see p79)*, hidden from view behind the main post office.

Afternoon

The road next to McDonald's leads to the **Marché Central** *(see p78)*, a worthwhile 15-minute detour. Return to Mohammed V for some of the best shopping in town, particularly around **Rue de la Liberté** *(see p78)*. The next major traffic intersection, Place Abdel Moumen Ben Ali, is overlooked by two pavement cafés: **Les Négociants** *(see p79)* and **Atlas** *(see p54)*; if you're after some authentic Moroccan food, try **Al Fassia** *(see p79)* on Boulevard Mohammed Zerktouni. You have the option of several good restaurants if you fancy a meal *(see p79)*. A taxi back to the medina will cost around 20 Dh.

Left **Café du Livre** Right **Al Badii**

TOP 10 Places to Shop

1 Scènes du Lin
Browse through the finely designed curtains with Fès embroidery and unusual lamps. *Map B5 • 70 rue de la Liberté • 0524 43 61 08 • Closed Aug • MC, V accepted*

2 Place Vendome
The leather items here are of greater quality than in the souks and are designed with an international flavour. *Map B5 • 141 ave Mohammed V • 0524 43 52 63 • Closed Jul–Aug • MC, V accepted*

3 Café du Livre
This haven for book lovers offers a range of interesting titles and a café with Wi-Fi access. *Map B5 • 44 rue Tarik Ben Ziad, next to Hotel Toulousain • 0524 43 21 49 • Closed Sun • Credit cards accepted*

4 Kenza Melehi
This designer gives a contemporary spin to traditional Moroccan patterns and fabrics. Glamorous and elegant garments. *Map B5 • 61 rue Yougoslavie, passage Ghandouri, Magasin 41, Guéliz • 0524 42 26 41 • Closed Sun • Credit cards accepted*

5 Galerie Birkmeyer
Good for leather goods or international designer sportswear. *Map B5 • 169–171 rue Mohammed El Bekal • 0524 44 69 63 • Closed 15 Jul–15 Aug • AmEx, MC, V accepted*

6 Marché Central
A variety of foodstuffs is available at this market, as well as handicrafts *(see p75)*.

7 Yahya
From small items to specially commissioned masterpieces, this young designer creates clothes of understated elegance. *Map B5 • 61 rue Yougoslavie, passage Ghandouri, Magasin 49, Guéliz • 0524 42 27 76 • Closed Sun • Credit cards accepted*

8 Atika Chaussures
Moccasins and loafers in myriad colours adorn this fashionable store. *Map B5 • 34 rue de la Liberté, Guéliz • 0524 43 64 09 • Closed Sun • Credit cards accepted*

9 L'Orientaliste
A small shop with small items like tea glasses and jewellery, its huge basement is packed with antique furniture. *Map B5 • 11 & 15 rue de la Liberté • 0524 43 40 74 • Closed Jul–Aug • MC, V accepted*

10 Al Badii
The best shop for unusual furnishings, ceramics, old embroidery, plus a basement full of carpets. Photos of celebrity shoppers hang on the walls. *Map B5 • 54 blvd Moulay Rachid • 0524 43 16 93 • Closed 1–15 Aug • Credit cards accepted*

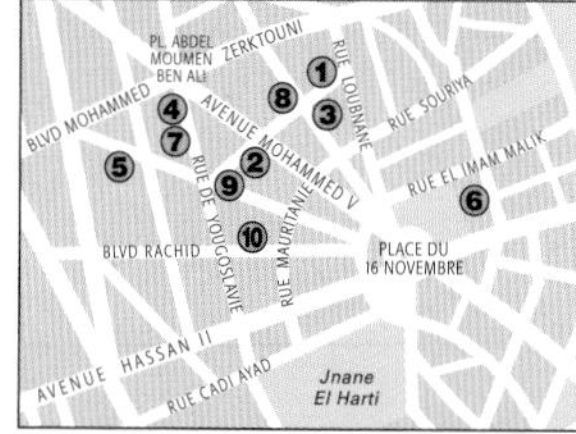

Most shops shut for two hours at lunch but open late into the evening; some are open Sunday mornings. Call ahead to check.

Comptoir

Price Categories

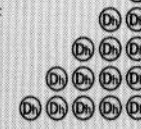

For a full meal for one with half a bottle of wine (or equivalent meal), plus taxes and extra charges.

Dh	under Dh100
Dh Dh	Dh100–200
Dh Dh Dh	Dh200–300
Dh Dh Dh Dh	Dh300–400
Dh Dh Dh Dh Dh	over Dh400

Top 10 Restaurants, Cafés and Bars

1 Kechmara

This hip bar-restaurant wouldn't look out of place in Paris. *Map B5 • 3 rue de la Liberté • 0524 42 25 32 • Open 7am–midnight Mon–Sat • MC, V accepted •* Dh Dh

2 Ultimo Bacio

This stylish restaurant conjures up the tastes of Italy. *Map B5 • Cnr rue Tarik Ben Ziad & Moulay Ali, Guéliz • 0661 11 26 09 • Open noon–2:30pm, 8–11pm daily (pm only on Sun) • Credit cards accepted •* Dh Dh Dh

3 Grand Café de la Poste

The high-deco interior of this café, built in 1925, is largely intact. The service can be patchy. *Map B5 • Cnr blvd El Mansour Eddahbi & ave Imam Malik • 0524 43 30 38 • Open 8am–1am daily • Credit cards accepted •* Dh Dh Dh

4 Rotisserie de la Paix

This grill restaurant with a lovely garden is a meat-eaters' delight. *Map B5 • 68 rue de Yougoslavie • 0524 43 31 18 • Open noon–3pm, 6:30–11pm daily • MC, V accepted •* Dh Dh

5 Restaurant Le Jacaranda

Indulge in French cuisine at this restaurant that doubles as an art gallery. *Map B5 • 32 bvd Mohammed Zerktouni • 0524 44 72 15 • Credit cards accepted •* Dh Dh Dh Dh

6 Al Fassia

Excellent, frill-free restaurant with a peaceful garden. *Map B5 • 55 blvd Mohammed Zerktouni • 0524 43 40 60 • Open noon–2:30pm, 7:30–11pm daily • Credit cards accepted •* Dh Dh Dh

7 Café du Livre

This bookshop also serves tea, coffee and simple meals. You can even enjoy a happy hour here *(see p78)*.

8 La Trattoria de Giancarlo

The city's best Italian restaurant is housed in a beautiful villa with seats beside the garden pool. *Map B5 • 179 rue Mohammed El Bekal • 0524 43 26 41 • Open 7:30–11:30pm daily; closed part of Jan • MC, V accepted •* Dh Dh Dh

9 Café Les Négociants

Stop at this popular café for tar-black coffee and gentle haggling with passing vendors. *Map B5 • Cnr ave Mohammed V & blv Mohammed Zerktouni • 0524 43 57 62 • Open from 8am daily • No credit cards •* Dh

10 Comptoir

Apart from the good food, Comptoir offers the unique Marrakech night out (if you like glamour and loud music). *Map C6 • Ave Echouhada • 0524 43 77 02 • Open 4pm–1am daily • MC, V accepted •* Dh Dh Dh

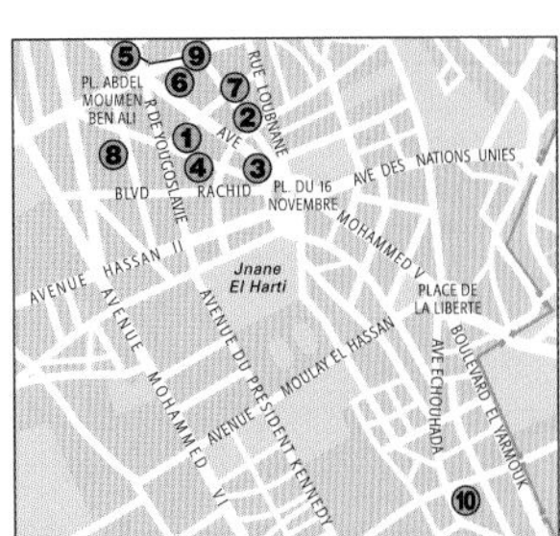

Displays at Galerie Damgaard

Essaouira

WHERE MARRAKECH IS A UNIFORM *pink, this sun-beaten town on the Atlantic coast is blue and white. The prosperity of the place peaked in the 18th and 19th centuries, when it was the most important port on the North African coast. It faded from consciousness in the 20th century, but drew plenty of travelling hippies in the 1960s and early 1970s. Its agreeably languid atmosphere is stirred only in late afternoon when the fishing fleet returns. Essaouira is known as the Wind City because of the constant winds.*

Left **The entrance to the port** Right **View of the ramparts along Skala de la Ville**

Top 10 Sights

1. Ramparts
2. Place Moulay Hassan
3. The port
4. The medina
5. The mellah
6. The souks
7. Place Orson Welles
8. The beaches
9. Galerie Damgaard
10. Musée des Arts et Traditions Populaires

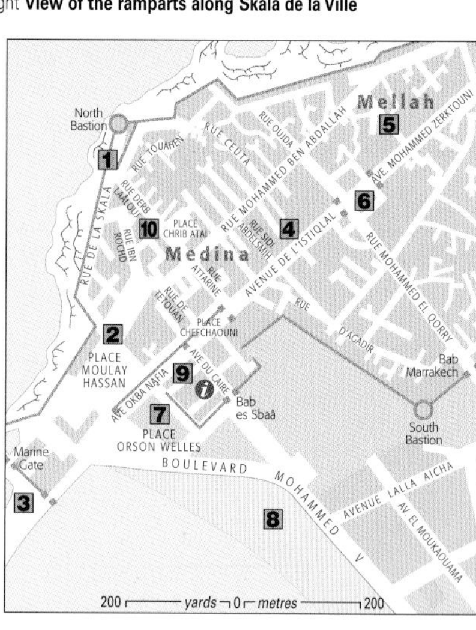

Supratours runs buses to Essaouira five times a day from its office, housed in the old train station. For more on Supratours, **see p104**.

Essaouira port

1 Ramparts

Essaouira's current layout can be traced back to 1765. That year, the town's local ruler captured a French ship and hired one of its passengers, an architect, to rebuild his port. He had the city surrounded with a heavy defensive wall, much of which still stands. The most impressive stretch is the Skala de la Ville, where you can walk along the top of the ramparts and examine several ancient cannons. *Map N1*

2 Place Moulay Hassan

Place Moulay Hassan is the focal point of Essaouira. A square in two parts, narrow and elongated to the north and opening out at the southern end, it lies between the medina proper and the port, and everybody passes through it at some point. It's lined by small cafés, where half the town seems to pass half of its time. *Map N2*

3 The port

Guarded by a toy-like, square fortress, Essaouira's port, the Skala du Port, is still a working concern complete with a boat yard, where vessels are still constructed out of wood. A daily market kicks into life between 3pm and 5pm with the arrival of the day's catch. Visitors can watch as the fish are auctioned off and follow that up by feasting on fresh sardines, grilled to order at the port end of Place Moulay Hassan. *Map N2*

4 The medina

As in Marrakech, Essaouira's medina is a labyrinth of narrow streets. It is, however, not as hard to navigate, bisected as it is by one long, straight street. This street begins at the port and runs all the way up to the north gate, the Bab Doukkala, undergoing two name changes along the way. *Map P1*

Place Moulay Hassan

5 The mellah

During the 18th and 19th centuries, a Jewish community gained prominence in Essaouira, becoming the most important economic group. They have all long since left and the town's Jewish quarter is in a dilapidated state. You can reach the mellah by following the alleys just inside the ramparts beyond Skala de la Ville. You can still identify the former Jewish residences, fronted as they are by balconies. In some cases, the Hebrew inscriptions on their lintels are also visible. *Map Q1*

6 The souks

At the heart of the medina is a lively market, the Souk Jdid, divided into four quarters by the intersection of two main thoroughfares. There is a daily souk for fish, spice and grains, and a cloistered square, known as the Joutia, where second-hand items are auctioned. *Map P1*

7 Place Orson Welles

Between the medina walls and the beach, a small park-like square goes by the name of Place Orson Welles, in honour of the great filmmaker who came to Essaouira in 1949 to shoot his version of *Othello*. Since then, Essaouira and the surrounding area have been used as movie locations in many international film projects, including Oliver Stone's epic *Alexander the Great* and Ridley Scott's *Kingdom of Heaven*. *Map N2–P2*

Music city

Essaouira was a popular hippy stopover in the late 1960s. Jimi Hendrix famously passed through, as did Frank Zappa. Cat Stevens, now Yusuf Islam, still returns each summer. The hippy influence lingers on: the annual Gnawa Festival d'Essaouira *(see p44)* attracts musicians from around the globe and has been described as the world's biggest jam session.

8 The beaches

Essaouira's beach, to the south of the medina, is one of the finest in Morocco. However, the strong winds that batter this part of the Atlantic coast frequently make it a little too

The spice souk

The beach at Essaouira

cold for comfort – not that this bothers the windsurfers or the boys who gather here to use the compact sand of the beach as a football pitch. ⊗ *Map P2*

9 Galerie Damgaard

For about a quarter of a century, a generation of painters and sculptors have made Essaouira an important centre of artistic activity. Many of these artists were brought to public attention by Dane Frederic Damgaard who used to run this influential gallery. ⊗ *Map P2 • Ave Oqba Bin Nafia, Medina • 0524 78 44 46 • Open 9am–1pm, 3–7pm daily www.galeriedamgaard.com*

10 Musée des Arts et Traditions Populaires

This small ethnographic museum occupies a 19th-century house that was formerly the town hall. It contains displays of ancient crafts, weapons and jewellery. Also displayed here are instruments and accessories that were used by religious brotherhoods. In addition you can also view some stunning examples of Berber and Jewish costumes. ⊗ *Map N1 • Rue Derb Laalouj, Medina • 0524 47 53 00 • Open 8:30am–noon, 2:30–6:30pm Wed–Mon*

A day by the sea

Morning

It is possible to do Essaouira as a day trip from Marrakech. You can get an early morning **CTM bus** from *gare routière (see p104)*, a Supratours coach at 8:30am or a ***grand taxi*** from a rank behind the bus station and arrive by 10am or 11am (although Essaouira is worth at least a couple of days). You will probably enter the city from the **Bab Marrakech** and follow Rue Mohammed El Qorry to the main crossroads of the medina, which is also the middle of the **souks**. Walk south down Avenue de L'Istiqlal, taking a right turn into shop-lined **Rue Attarine**. A first left leads down to **Place Moulay Hassan** *(see p81)*, a great place for a snack at one of the many cafés. Follow the squawks of the seagulls south to the **port** *(see p81)* and a lunch of grilled sardines.

Afternoon

From the port, backtrack to Place Moulay Hassan but take a left at the famed **Taros** café *(see p85)* and follow the narrow alley, **Rue de la Skala**, on the inside of the high sea wall. There are some wood-carving workshops here. After a short walk, a ramp leads up to the **ramparts** *(see p81)* for a wonderful view. Descend and then continue to the **mellah**, the old Jewish quarter. Find your way back to the souks and again follow Avenue de L'Istiqlal south. Take a left along Avenue du Caire, exiting by the Bab Es Sbâa and turning right for the **beach**. The **Chalet de la Plage** *(see p85)* is perfect for an early (or late) dinner by the ocean.

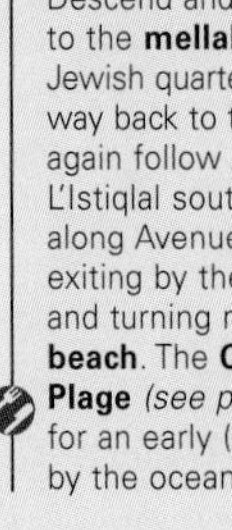

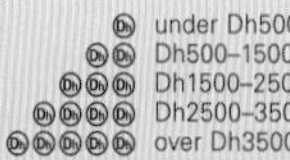

Price Categories

For a standard double room per night with taxes and breakfast if included.

Dh	under Dh500
DhDh	Dh500–1500
DhDhDh	Dh1500–2500
DhDhDhDh	Dh2500–3500
DhDhDhDhDh	over Dh3500

Left **Villa Maroc** Right **Riad Al Medina**

Top 10 Places to Stay

1 Palazzo Desdemona

Room sizes vary but it's got atmosphere and offers excellent value. *Map P2 • 12–14 rue Youssef El Fassi • 0524 47 22 27 • www.palazzodesdemona.com • DhDh*

2 Riad Al Medina

The former Hippy Café, supposedly frequented by Jimi Hendrix, restored as a charming riad. *Map P2 • 9 rue El Attarine • 0524 47 59 07 • www.riadalmadina.com • DhDh*

3 Riad Nakhla

All rooms have en-suite bathrooms and there's a courtyard with a fountain and a terrific roof terrace. *Map P2 • 12 rue d'Agadir • 0524 47 49 40 • www.essaouiranet.com/riad-nakhla • Dh*

4 Lalla Mira

This solar-powered eco-hotel has an organic restaurant and a hotel farm. Guests get free use of the *hammam* next door. *Map Q2 • 14 rue d'Algerie • 0524 47 50 46 • www.lallamira.net • DhDhDhDhDh*

5 Dar Adul

This cosy house has five bedrooms, a sitting room and a roof terrace. *Map N1 • 63 rue Touahen • 0524 47 39 10 • www.dar-adul.com • DhDh*

6 Dar Loulema

Perfectly located just off Place Moulay Hassan, this is a popular old home with chic decor. It has eight rooms around a central courtyard. *Map N2 • 2 rue Souss • 0524 47 53 46 • www.darloulema.com • DhDh*

7 Dar El Bahar

Located beside the northern ramparts, with the waves pounding below, the best rooms have glorious sea views. *Map P1 • 1 rue Touahen • 0524 47 68 31 • www.daralbahar.com • DhDh*

8 Villa Maroc

Essaouira's first boutique hotel was built by knocking together four houses. It has friendly, efficient staff and fine views from the roof terraces. *Map P2 • 10 rue Abdellah Ben Yassine • 0524 47 61 47 • www.villa-maroc.com • DhDhDh*

9 Sofitel Mogador

Apart from the usual luxuries of a five-star hotel, you can also indulge in thalassotherapy treatments that use marine minerals. *Map Q3 • Avenue Mohammed V • 0524 47 90 00 • www.sofitel.com • DhDhDhDh*

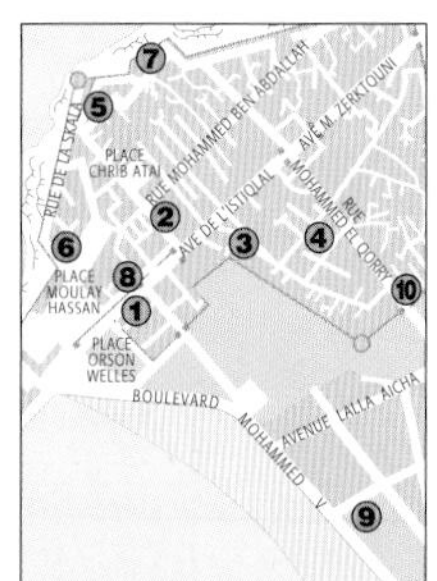

10 L'Heure Bleue

This hotel has colonial-style rooms and all the facilities you could want: a screening room, a pool and the medina's only lift. *Map Q2 • 2 rue Ibn Batouta • 0524 78 34 34 • www.heure-bleue.com • DhDhDhDh*

Villa Maroc, Sofitel Mogador and L'Heure Bleue all accept credit cards.

Price Categories

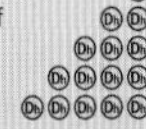

For a full meal for one with half a bottle of wine (or equivalent meal), plus taxes and extra charges.	
Dh	under Dh100
DhDh	Dh100–200
DhDhDh	Dh200–300
DhDhDhDh	Dh300–400
DhDhDhDhDh	over Dh400

Left **Taros** Right **A port-side fish stall**

TOP 10 Places to Eat and Drink

1 Port-side fish stalls

The best meal in Essaouira is seafood fresh off the boat, grilled and eaten at a group of stalls on the port side of Place Moulay Hassan. *Map N2 • Place Moulay Hassan • 0524 78 40 33 • Dh*

2 Chalet de la Plage

This beachside restaurant has a wonderful sea-facing open terrace. Wine and beer are served. *Map N2 • 1 ave M'hamed V • 0524 47 59 72 • Open noon–1:30pm, 6:30–9pm Mon–Sat • Credit cards accepted • DhDh*

3 Chez Sam

This boat-shaped shack sits at the harbour's end. It's great for watching the boats come into the harbour to deliver the catch – part of which will end up as your meal. *Map N2 • Port de Pêche • 0524 47 62 38 • Open 12:30–3pm, 7:30–10pm daily • MC, V accepted • DhDhDh*

4 Taros

Sip a drink on the terrace at sunset, staring out to sea, then enjoy the mix of Moroccan and French dishes. Live music most nights. *Map N2 • Place Moulay Hassan • 0524 47 64 07 • Open 11am–4pm, 6pm–midnight Mon–Sat • Credit cards accepted • DhDhDh www.taroscafe.com*

5 Ferdaous

Cosy place serving traditional, seasonal Moroccan cuisine. Prices are cheap and the place is hugely popular, so book in advance. *Map P2 • 27 rue Abdessalam Lebad • 0524 47 36 55 • Open 12:30–3pm, 7:30–11pm daily • Dh*

6 Les Alizés Mogador

This restaurant beside the ramparts serves hearty portions of Moroccan food. *Map N1 • 26 rue de la Skala • 0524 47 68 19 • Open noon–3:30pm, 7:30–11pm daily • DhDh*

7 Silvestro

This unpretentious Italian restaurant has a short list of Italian wines. *Map N1 • 70 rue Laâlouj • 0524 47 35 55 • Open 11:30am–3pm, 7–11pm daily (closed Wed pm) • DhDh*

8 Chez Driss

Since 1928 this patisserie has been serving cakes, coffee and juices to locals and visitors alike. *Map N2 • 10 rue El Hajali • 0524 47 57 93 • Open 7am–10pm daily • Dh*

9 Côté Plage

Part of the Sofitel complex, this beachfront café serves tapas and barbecues. *Map Q3 • Blvd M'hamed V • 0524 47 90 00 • DhDhDh*

10 Restaurant El Minzah

A popular place for a good meal in a relaxed atmosphere. *Map N2 • 3 ave Okba Ibnou Nafia • 0524 47 53 08 • Open noon–3pm, 6:30–11pm daily • DhDhDh*

The precarious highway hugging the Atlas Mountains

Tizi-n-Test Pass

THE HIGH-ALTITUDE TIZI-N-TEST PASS, *the westerly of the two great passes over the Atlas Mountains, is cautiously navigated by the R203 highway to Taroudant. Although the distance between the two cities is only 223 km (138 miles), the road's tortuous hairpins demand such respect from drivers that the journey takes nearly five hours. Not to mention the time needed to stop off at the many sights along the way. If you don't have your own vehicle or* grand taxi, *you can make the trip by public transport: buses depart Marrakech early each morning, taking up to eight hours to reach Taroudant.*

View up Ait Mizane valley to Kasbah Tamadot near Asni

Sights

1. Tahanoute
2. Moulay Brahim
3. Asni
4. Jbel Toubkal
5. Ouirgane
6. Kasbah Talaat-n-Yacoub
7. Tin Mal
8. Tizi-n-Test Pass
9. Taroudant
10. Tichka Plateau

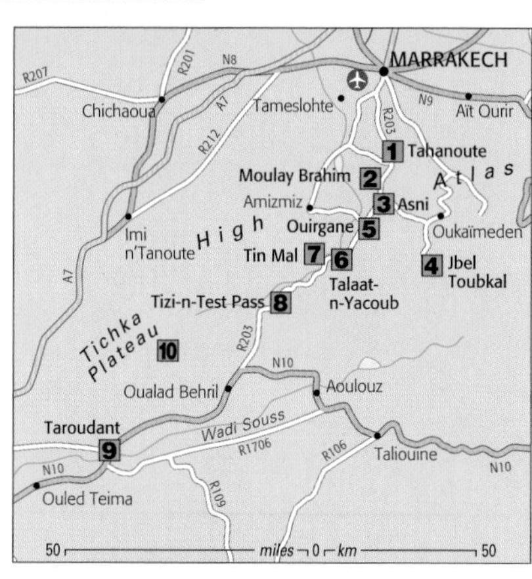

Preceding pages **Kasbah Aït Benhaddou**

1 Tahanoute

This administrative centre is just a 20-minute drive south of Marrakech. The old village has a cascade of red clay houses, surrounding a massive rock sheltering the shrine of Sidi Mohammed El Kebir, whose festival is celebrated at Mouloud, the Prophet's birthday. It was the subject of Winston Churchill's last painting in 1958. Every Tuesday, a country market is held here. *Map C1*

2 Moulay Brahim

South of Tahanoute, the road winds uphill to Moulay Brahim, named after a local saint, with a green-roofed shrine dedicated to him in the middle of the village (entry to non-Muslims is forbidden). The shrine is a popular pilgrimage spot, especially for women with fertility problems. *Map C2*

3 Asni

The village of Asni lies at a fork in the road – a left turn leads up to the village of Imlil and the striking kasbahs Tamadot and Toubkal *(see p56)*. Jbel Toubkal dominates the view to the west, but there's little for visitors to explore at Asni itself, apart from shops selling trinkets (things are cheaper in Marrakech). The highlight is the busy country market held on Saturdays – the largest in the Atlas. *Map C2*

Entrance to the Asni market

4 Jbel Toubkal

Take the left fork at Asni to Imlil at the foot of Jbel Toubkal, North Africa's highest peak. Mountain guides can be hired in Imlil at the *bureau des guides* in the centre of the village. There are some basic budget hotels here, but the Kasbah du Toubkal just up the hill is a better option *(see p93)*. *Map C2 • Bureau des guides: tel/fax 0524 48 56 26*

The red clay houses of the old village of Tahanoute

Argan Oil

The precious Argan trees, similar in appearance to olive trees, are found only in southwestern Morocco. They bear a fruit from which oil can be extracted by splitting, roasting and pressing the nuts. Locals use it as a medicine; it's also a staple of beauty and massage treatments and tastes delicious when it's drizzled on couscous.

5 Ouirgane

Ouirgane, 16 km (10 miles) south of Asni, is a pretty little place. The actual village is hidden among the trees along the valley above the Oued Nifis river. There's a Jewish saint's shrine and two salt factories (one modern, one traditional). Stop by for lunch or, if you plan on lingering in the village, why not spend the night at the Au Sanglier Qui Fume *(see p93)* – for which the place is best known. *Map C2*

Argan fruit

6 Kasbah Talaat-n-Yacoub

South of Ouirgane, the road climbs steadily through a rocky, bare landscape. After passing through the small Berber hamlet of Ijoujak, visible off to the right is the commanding hilltop fortress of Kasbah Talaat-n-Yacoub. This was once a stronghold of the Goundafi tribe who controlled access to the Tizi-n-Test until the early 20th century, when they were subdued by the French. *Map C2*

7 Tin Mal

The main attraction at Tin Mal is an ancient mosque that dates back to the time of the Almohads *(see p32)*. Way back in the 12th century, this was the heart of a mountain empire that had unified local tribes under a militant version of Islam. It was from here that an army set out in 1144 to lay siege to Marrakech and went on to conquer the rest of Morocco. This restored mosque provided the basic architectural prototype for the impressive Koutoubia in Marrakech. Though roofless, it continues to be the venue for Friday prayers, the one day when it remains inaccessible to visitors. *Map C2 • Closed Fridays • Adm*

8 Tizi-n-Test Pass

How much you enjoy the experience of this 2,092-m (6,861-ft) pass depends on whether you are a passenger or in the driver's seat. As a driver, you have to keep your eyes glued to the road ahead in order to negotiate the endless hairpin bends. The narrow road with no safety barriers ensures that you won't have much opportunity to enjoy the spectacular views. But for passengers, the view across

Tin Mal Mosque interior

Souvenir shops along the Tizi-n-Test Pass

the plains of the Sous to the south is beautiful. There are various souvenir stalls and small cafés located on the pass itself where you can stop and enjoy the panorama. *Map B2*

9 Taroudant

Built on the proceeds of gold brought from the Sahara, Taroudant was the capital of the Saadian dynasty early in the 16th century. Today, enclosed within reddish-yellow walls, it resembles a smaller, sleepier version of Marrakech. It features a grand kasbah that can be reached by passing under the triple-arched Saadian Gates, as well as some foul-smelling tanneries. You will also find two excellent souks here, including the Arab Souk, with its focus on traditional crafts. *Map B2*

10 Tichka Plateau

A highland plateau of beautiful meadows, the Tichka Plateau is found to the north of Taroudant. Particularly striking in spring when the wild flowers are in full bloom, it's a fine place to go trekking but best enjoyed with qualified guides. Go to the *bureau des guides* in Imlil *(see p89)* to arrange for one. *Map B2*

A Day in Taroudant

Morning

Though **Taroudant** resembles a more ramshackle Marrakech at first sight, it has more of an African than Arab identity. Unlike most other Moroccan cities, it was never under French occupation and so doesn't possess a European quarter. Begin your exporation of the city on **Place El Alaouyine**, known by its Berber name as Place Assarag. Follow **Avenue Mohammed V** south of the square and head east into **Souk Arabe**, famed for its antique shops. At the souk's edge, **Boulangerie El Widad** offers tasty Moroccan pastries. South of the main street, across Place El Nasr is **Souk Berbère** the main fruit and vegetable market. Return north up Ave Bir Anzarené and take a right on Avenue Moulay Rachid; sample the tajines at **Chez Nada**.

Afternoon

As you walk east on Avenue Moulay Rachid through an orange-tree-lined path, you will come upon the triple-arched Saadian Gates at **Bab El Kasbah**. These lead to the walled **kasbah quarter** built by Mohammed ech-Cheikh who made it the capital of the Saadian empire. The poorest part of town, it used to house the governor's palace, now the very chic **Hotel Palais Salam** *(see p93)*. Stop at the hotel for a snack and then make your way back to the Bab El Kasbah. Hop into one of the waiting *calèches* and for a small fee, do a circuit of the city walls. You can take the *calèche* back to Place El Alaouyine or your hotel.

Left **Sous Massa National Park** Right **Saffron flowers at Taliouine**

TOP 10 West to the Coast

1 Tioute Kasbah

About 37 km (23 miles) southeast of Taroudant, the imposing Tioute Kasbah (containing a restaurant) dominates a palm grove. This was the location for the film *Ali Baba and the Forty Thieves* in 1954. *Map B3*

2 The Atlas Mountains

The peaks of the western High Atlas – particularly Jbel Aoulime, at a height of 3,555 m (11,667 ft) – can be reached via road 7020 north of Taroudant. *Map B2*

3 Taliouine

Taliouine, a town with a ruined kasbah once owned by the Glaoui clan *(see pp32 & 96)*, is also the world's biggest saffron growing area. *Map C2*

4 Tazenakht

In Tazenakht, beneath the Jbel Siroua peak, carpets with an orange weft are woven by the Ouaouzgite tribe. *Map C2*

5 The Anti-Atlas

As the R106 from Taliouine crosses the Anti-Atlas, at the 94-km (58-mile) mark, Igherm is a large mountain village with women clad in all black and coloured headbands. *Map C3*

6 Tafraoute

At an altitude of 1,200 m (3,938 ft), Tafraoute stands in the heart of a stunning valley in the Anti-Atlas. The palm groves here are lush and when they flower in February, the almond trees are covered with clouds of pink and white blossom. *Map B3*

7 Tiznit

A small town surrounded by pink *pisé* ramparts, you feel the proximity of both the Atlantic and the desert here. Its central *méchouar* parade ground is lined with cafés and shops. *Map A3*

8 Sidi Ifni

This colonial-style town sits on the crest of a rocky plateau overlooking the Atlantic. Follow the coast road after Tiznit.

9 Sous Massa National Park

The park along the banks of Wadi Massa contains reed beds inhabited by flamingoes and the endangered bald ibis. *Map A3*

10 Agadir

Flattened by an earthquake in 1960, Agadir was rebuilt and is now a thriving charter tourist resort. The grim aspect of the town is compensated by its fantastic beaches. *Map A3*

• Tourist information: Ave du Prince Moulay Abdallah • 0528 84 63 77

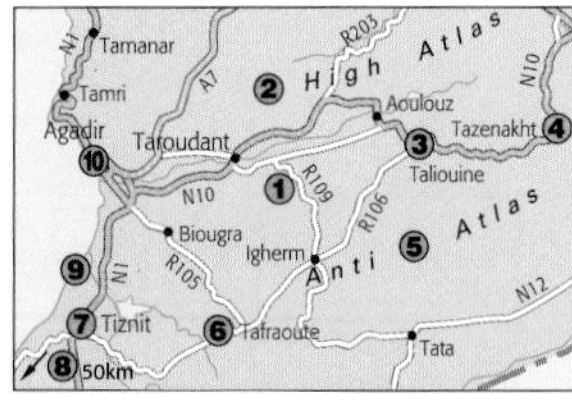

Gazelle d'Or

Price Categories

For a standard double room per night with taxes and breakfast if included.		
	Dh	under Dh500
	DhDh	Dh500–1500
	DhDhDh	Dh1500–2500
	DhDhDhDh	Dh2500–3500
	DhDhDhDhDh	over Dh3500

Top 10 Places to Stay

1 Le Palais Oumensour

Well located for those who wish to explore Taroudant on foot, this hotel has simple but comfortable rooms and is great value for money. *Map B2 • Burj Al Mansour Oumensour Tadjount, Taroudant • 0528 55 02 15 • www.palaisoumensour.com • No credit cards •* DhDh

2 Au Sanglier Qui Fume

Steeped in local history, this friendly inn once quartered the French Foreign Legion soldiers who built the bridge over the Ouirgane river. *Map C2 • Ouirgane • 0524 48 57 07 • www.ausanglierquifume.com • No credit cards •* Dh

3 Kasbah Tamadot

At the foothills of the Atlas Mountains, this stunning kasbah belongs to British entrepreneur Richard Branson. *Map C2 • BP67, Asni • 0524 36 82 00 • www.virgin.com/kasbah • Credit cards accepted •* DhDhDhDhDh

4 Kasbah du Toubkal

This beautifully restored kasbah in the shadow of North Africa's highest peak is a great base for trekking. *Map C2 • BP31, Imlil • 0524 48 56 11 • www.kasbahdutoubkal.com •* DhDhDh

5 Hotel Taroudant

A fading institution, it still offers the best budget beds in town. The hotel also organizes mountain treks. *Map B2 • Place El Alaouyine, Assarag, Taroudant • 0528 85 24 16 •* DhDh

6 Hotel Palais Salam

Sheltered within Taroudant's fortress walls, the hotel was once the palace of a *pasha* (provincial governor) and boasts ornate Moorish interiors and lush Andalusian gardens. *Map B2 • Ave Moulay Ismail, BP 258, Taroudant • 0528 85 25 01 •* DhDhDh

7 Gazelle d'Or

Outside Taroudant, this former Belgian baron's hunting lodge has been converted into a hotel with 30 grand bungalows set in enormous grounds. *Map B2 • 83000 Taroudant • 0528 85 20 39 •* DhDhDhDhDh

8 Auberge Souktana

A family-run auberge just outside Taliouine. Accommodation is in four small bungalows; not all rooms have their own showers. Tented accommodation is available in the gardens. *Map C2 • Opposite Kasbah Laglaoui, Taliouine • 0528 53 40 75 •* Dh–DhDh

9 Hotel Idou Tiznit

Notable for its location rather than its decor, this hotel is ideal for those on a limited budget. *Map A3 • Ave Hassan II, Tiznit • 0528 60 03 33 • www.idoutiznit.com • Credit cards accepted •* DhDh

10 Hotel Les Amandiers

Although it could do with sprucing up, Les Amandiers makes a good base for exploring the region. *Map B3 • BP 10 Centre de Tafraoute • 0528 80 00 88 •* DhDh

Kasbah Taourirt

Tizi-n-Tichka Pass

THE N9 HIGHWAY RUNS FROM *Marrakech southeast over the Atlas Mountains, crossing the country's highest pass. On the other side, it then descends to the town of Ouarzazate, considered to be the gateway to the Sahara. Along this route, you will come across some interesting sights, including the kasbahs of Telouet and Aït Benhaddou (both off the main road). From start to finish, the route is 196 km (122 miles) on a good road. However, there are some tortuous stretches that demand careful driving; as a result, the journey invariably takes nearly four hours. Travellers can arrange for a* grand taxi *or hire a car. Alternatively, several Ouarzazate buses travel this route daily from Marrakech's main bus station. Supratours runs daily trips to Ouarzazate.*

Left **Vehicles navigating the twisting road over the pass** Right **Ouarzazate**

Sights

1. Aït Ourir
2. Taddert
3. Tizi-n-Tichka Pass
4. Kasbah Telouet
5. Aït Benhaddou
6. Kasbah Tiffoultoute
7. Ouarzazate
8. Kasbah Taourirt
9. Atlas Corporation Studios
10. Horse and Camel Fantasias

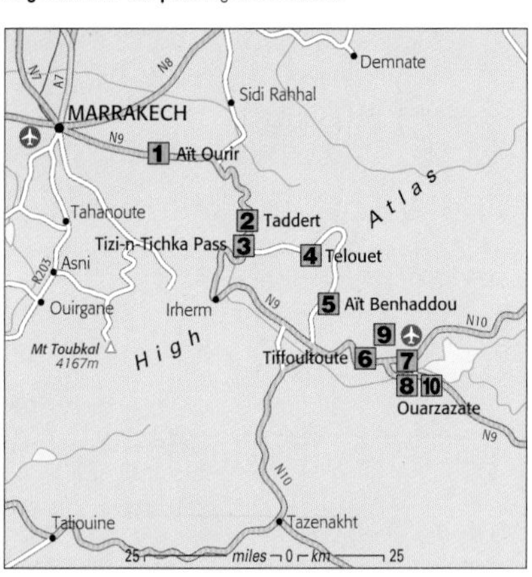

Reception room of Kasbah Telouet

1 Aït Ourir

This busy little rural town 35 km (22 miles) outside Marrakech becomes even more active on Fridays, when it hosts a weekly country market. If you choose to pass through on the right day, it makes for a great hour-long stop off. Ⓢ *Map C1*

2 Taddert

After Aït Ourir, the road starts to climb. The last halt before the pass is the busy village of Taddert, set among walnut groves. In the higher part of the settlement, a handful of good cafés offer views of the valley below. When the pass is closed by bad weather, a barrier is lowered here to halt all south-bound traffic. Ⓢ *Map C1*

Aït Ourir

3 Tizi-n-Tichka Pass

As the road leaves Taddert the greenery comes to an end and the landscape turns scenically barren and rugged. The twisting road with precipitous drops will keep drivers' eyes firmly fixed on the road. At its highest point, the pass peaks at 2,260 m (7,415 ft), marked by no more than a few stalls selling colourful rocks found in the region, although some of these are fake. When broken, they reveal glittering crystal formations within. Ⓢ *Map C2*

4 Kasbah Telouet

Telouet, the stronghold of the Glaoui tribe who, in the early 20th century, came to rule all of southern Morocco under French sponsorship, is a village dominated by a magnificent kasbah. Abandoned for nearly half a century, much of the structure is crumbling and dangerous, but you can visit the ornate reception hall and the rooftop terrace, which gives stunning views. Ⓢ *Map C2 • Adm*

Thami El Glaoui

In 1893, the Glaoui tribe of Telouet was rewarded for rescuing Sultan Moulay Hassan and his army from a raging blizzard, and benefited further after the French took over. Thami El Glaoui was then made *pasha* (lord), one of the most powerful men in the country. Hated for his support of the French, he died soon after Morocco gained independence.

5 Aït Benhaddou

This kasbah is on UNESCO's list of World Heritage Sites and is one of the best preserved of all the kasbahs in the region. It is also the most famous, thanks to its popularity with visiting film producers, and has been immortalized in dozens of movies, including *Lawrence of Arabia*, *The Last Temptation of Christ*, *The Mummy*, *Gladiator* and *Alexander*. Part of the appeal lies in the location: the kasbah tumbles down a hillside beside the Ouarzazate River. It is still partially inhabited by ten families. *Map D2*

Kasbah Aït Benhaddou

6 Kasbah Tiffoultoute

Tiffoultoute is another kasbah that once belonged to the Glaoui and is situated just outside of Ouarzazate. Although parts of it are crumbling away, another section has been rebuilt and serves as a hotel and restaurant. The location is beautiful, situated dramatically between a river and a palm oasis. *Map D2 • Open 8am–7pm daily*

7 Ouarzazate

The so-called "Gateway to the Sahara" (pronounced "war-zazat") is a town of around 60,000 people. Most visitors tend to spend at least one night here before pushing on south to the desert proper *(see "South to the Desert", right)* or heading east to the Dadès Valley and beyond *(see p98)*. The number of hotels in town is always increasing and with constantly improving quality. There are plenty of interesting activities here, from camel-trekking and quad biking to visiting the film studios for which the town is renowned *(see below)*. *Map D2 • Tourist Office: 0524 88 24 85*

8 Kasbah Taourirt

This is the main landmark of Ouarzazate, a large kasbah that used to belong to the Glaoui tribe. Parts are still inhabited, while some abandoned sections have been carefully restored. A pleasant place to wander through, its atmospheric, narrow alleys evoke a real sense of what life in the kasbah was like in the past. *Map D2 • Open 8:30am–6pm daily • Adm*

9 Atlas Corporation Studios

A busy, administrative hub of a region with spectacular mountain and desert scenery,

Pharaonic props at Atlas Studios

Ouarzazate has become the centre of the Moroccan film industry and is also home to the Atlas Corporation Studios, 6 km (4 miles) north of town. They were built specifically to provide some infrastructure, including sound stages and sets, for movies. Films shot here include *Gladiator* and *Kingdom of Heaven*. It's well worth dropping in to see sets like the Tibetan monastery built for *Kundun* and Egyptian temple sets from French production, *Asterix and Cleopatra*. A yellow bus shuttles between the studio and Ouarzazate's main street, Avenue Mohammed V. *Map D2*
• 0524 88 22 12 • Open 8:30–5pm daily
• Guided tours last 30–40 mins • Adm
• www.studiosatlas.com

10 Horse and Camel Fantasias

A company called North Africa Horse, known for its choreography of charges and equestrian stunts for many of the "sword-and-sandal" adventure films, also puts on horse and camel shows for tourists. Watch recreations of famous scenes from movies such as *Kingdom of Heaven* and *Alexander* over dinner. Call for details. *Map D2 • Route de Skoura, km 20 from Ouarzazate, next to Golf Royal • 0524 88 66 90/0661 16 84 72*

South to the Desert

Day One

From **Ouarzazate**, the road continues south through the **Drâa Valley** down to the administrative town of **Zagora**. A drive of about four hours, stop over at **Tamnougalt**, a dramatic *ksar* (fortified village) 10 minutes off the main road, 5 km (3 miles) after the small market town of Agdz. Further south is the Glaoui-era **Kasbah Timiderte**. Zagora itself is dominated by **Jbel Zagora**, a rocky outcrop at the town's end. The lively market held on Wednesday and Sunday teems with dates, grown in abundance here. Just south of the centre is the pretty hamlet of **Amezrou**. Nearby, the **Kasbah des Juifs** is inhabited by Berber silversmiths (the Jews who lived here are long gone). Zagora's most famous attraction is at the town's exit: a sign with a camel caravan that simply reads, "Timbuktu, 52 Days".

Day Two

The village of M'Hamid is 96 km (60 miles) further south of Zagora. En route, **Tamegroute's** mosque-and-shrine complex is off limits to non-Muslims, except for the library with its collection of ancient manuscripts. Five kilometres (3 miles) further on, you will see the first of the sand dunes at **Tinfou**. The best dunes, however, can be accessed from **M'Hamid**, a sleepy outpost at the road's end – a one-street settlement, it feels like it's at the end of the world. Desert trips, from excursions of a few hours, to expeditions lasting several days, can be arranged from here.

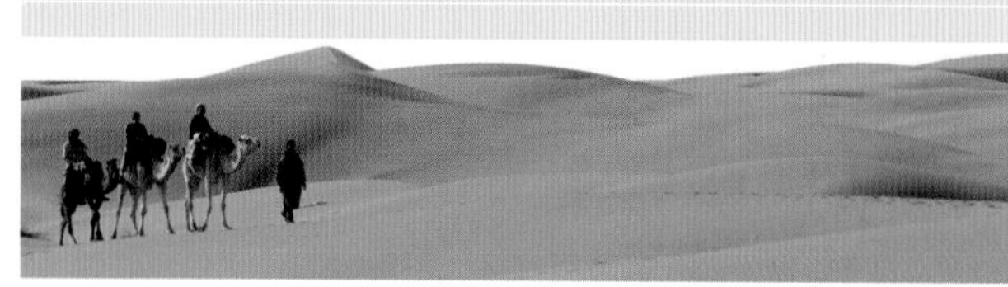

Camels trekking at Erg Chebbi dunes

TOP 10 The Valley of the Kasbahs

1 Skoura
The first town east of Ouarzazate is notable for a palmeraie with impressive old kasbahs, including the Kasbah Amerhidil (part hotel, part museum), once owned by the Glaoui family *(see p96)*. *Map D2*

2 El Kelaa M'Gouna
This small town lies at the heart of rose-growing country. Most of the petals picked each spring are exported for use in the perfume industry. *Map D2*

3 Dadès Gorge
Follow the road north from Boumalne du Dadès to this stunning gorge, a spectacular backdrop for several kasbahs. *Map E1*

4 Tinerhir
Built on a rocky outcrop, the region's administrative centre is bordered by lush palm groves. Known for its silver jewellery, it has several working silver mines nearby. *Map E1 • Tourist information: Hotel Tombouctou; 0544 83 46 04*

5 Todra Gorge
Sheer cliffs dramatically rise on either side of this narrow gorge with the picturesque village of Tamtattouchte at the northern end. Two hotels make an overnight stay possible. *Map E1*

6 Goulmina
The fortified villages, or *ksours*, here were built to provide a strong defence against the pillaging nomads. A walled settlement east of the Erfoud road is worth a detour. *Map E1*

7 Er Rachidia
From this town, the extensive palm groves of Ziz and Tafilalt begin. The place is known for crafts such as pottery and carved wooden objects. *Map F1*
• Tourist information: 0535 57 09 44

8 Erfoud
This peaceful town serves as a base for tours to the soaring Erg Chebbi sand dunes and the Tafilalt palm grove. It also hosts a three-day Date Festival each October following the annual date harvest. *Map F1*

9 Rissani
This ancient town dating back to the 7th century lies on the edge of the Sahara and has a very famous souk. *Map F1*

10 Merzouga
This is a Saharan oasis at the foot of the Erg Chebbi dunes. Camel drivers offer one-hour to two-day tours into the sand hills. *Map F2*

Kasbah Aït Ben Moro

Price Categories

For a standard double room per night with taxes and breakfast if included.	
Dh	under Dh500
DhDh	Dh500–1500
DhDhDh	Dh1500–2500
DhDhDhDh	Dh2500–3500
DhDhDhDhDh	over Dh3500

Top 10 Places to Stay

1 Auberge Telouet

A budget auberge in the traditional style. The walls are made of huge stones, and rooms are spartan but attractive. Not all rooms have en-suite facilities. *Map C2 • Telouet • 0524 89 07 17 • www.telouet.com • No credit cards •* Dh

2 Irocha

Midway between Telouet and Aït Benhaddou, this hotel has charming touches, such as a telescope on the roof for stargazing. It also has a pool and a *hammam*. *Map C2 • Tisselday • 0667 73 70 02 • www.irocha.com • No credit cards •* DhDh

3 Hotel la Kasbah

Across the river from the kasbah, with a small pool. The basic rooms are best described as "desert chic". *Map D2 • Aït Benhaddou • 0524 89 03 02 •* DhDh *• www.hotel-la-kasbah.com*

4 Dar Daif

This intimate 12-room guest house, 5km from the town centre, has a *hammam*, a pool and a bedroom equipped for disabled guests. *Map D2 • Route de Zagora, Ouarzazate • 0524 85 49 49 • www.dardaif.ma •* DhDh

5 Le Berbère Palace

One of the three luxury hotels in Ouarzazate, it boasts air-conditioned bungalows, large pool, *hammam*, solarium and tennis courts. *Map D2 • Quartier Mansour Eddahabi • 0524 88 31 05 • www.le-berbere-palace.hotel-m.com •* DhDhDhDh

6 Kasbah Aït Ben Moro

At night, this 18th-century fortress with thick walls and a palm-tree garden is lit by lanterns, creating a cosy atmosphere. *Map D2 • Skoura • 0524 85 21 16 • www.aitbenmoro.com • No credit cards •* DhDh

7 Dar Ahlam

This is a kasbah transformed into a palatial boutique hotel complete with a library, *hammam* and use of a 4-wheel drive and driver. *Map D2 • Douar Oulad, Chakh Ali, Skoura • 0524 85 22 39 • www.darahlam.com •* DhDhDhDh

8 Kasbah Lamrani

This small kasbah, with 22 air-conditioned rooms, is a good base for a trip to the Todra Gorge 15 km (7 miles) away. *Map E1 • Zone Touristique, blvd Mohammed V, Tinerhir • 0524 83 50 17 • www.kasbahlamrani.com •* DhDh

9 Kasbah Xaluca

A large place within a walled enclosure with a big swimming pool, it is tailored to suit groups and even has DJs at night. *Map F1 • Erfoud • 0535 57 84 50 • www.xaluca.com •* DhDh

10 Hotel Kenzi Belere

This four-star hotel, just outside Erfoud, is easily the area's best. The 140 air-conditioned rooms, all equipped with satellite television, are arranged off the swimming pool garden. *Map F1 • Route de Rissani, Erfoud • 0535 57 81 90 •* DhDhDh

Following pages **Stalls at Jemaa El Fna**

LAVENDE

STREETSMART

Getting There 102

Planning Your Trip 103

Getting Around 104

Useful Information 105

Etiquette 106

Things to Avoid 107

Security and Health 108

Shopping and Eating 109

Accommodation Tips 110

International and Chain Hotels 111

Hostels and Other Cheapies 112

Budget but Chic 113

Mid-range Riads 114–115

Luxury Riads and Hotels 116

The Palmeraie and Further Afield 117

Left **Reaching Marrakech by air** Right **The local railway station**

Top 10 Getting There

1 Airlines

Marrakech is most easily accessible by air. Royal Air Maroc (royalairmaroc.com) is the national airline, with regular international services. Jet4You (Jetfly.com) and Ryanair (Ryanair.com) also have flights from some British airports. British Airways (britishairways.com) also flies to Marrakech.

2 Air fares

Since budget airlines began services to the city, it has become remarkably cheap to travel there. Fares from London Gatwick, Stansted and Luton airports start from as low as £1 one way plus taxes.

3 Marrakech International Airport

Just 4 km (2 miles) from the centre of town, the formerly modest airport has been significantly expanded in order to accommodate the vast number of flights. The drive into the city takes under 10 minutes. The number 19 bus will take you into town for 30 Dh.

4 Airport taxis

Taxis gather in the car park outside the Arrivals terminal. Even though all taxis have meters, they are never switched on for the airport run. A ride that would normally cost 30 Dh can cost more than 100 Dh.

5 By train

The modern train station receives daily services from Rabat, Casablanca and Tangier. If you have time and money to spare, you can take the Eurostar from London to Paris, and then the daily TGV service to Algeciras in Spain. From Algeciras it's a ferry ride to Tangier. There are no public lavatories in Marrakech, and the station has the only free facilities.

6 By bus

The national bus company, CTM, running locally and out of town, is the best. Supratours runs buses between Marrakech, Essaouira and many other destinations.

7 *Grands taxis*

These shared taxis gather on Marché du Mellah and at the *gare routière*. They connect Marrakech with Casablanca, Fès and Essaouira. All the fares are fixed; just turn up and take a seat. Alternatively, hire one of your own and get it to take you wherever you want.

8 By car

There are frequent ferry services operating between France, Spain and north Morocco. A motorway links Tangier with Marrakech and continues on to Agadir, connecting with an improved road to Essaouira.

9 Organized tours

Numerous companies offer Morocco packages and most include stays in Marrakech. Best of Morocco (www.morocco-travel.com) is UK-based; Marrakesh Voyage (www.morocco-travel-agency.com) is US-based; Yallah (www.yallahmorocco.com) is a national operator.

10 The tunnel

In 2006, Lombardi Engineers (Swiss) were retained to build the ambitious tunnel connecting Spain and Morocco. The tunnel is expected to be completed by 2025.

Directory

Jet4You
Marrakech Menara Airport
• 0890 40 44 04

Marrakech Menara Airport
• 0524 44 79 10

Royal Air Maroc
• 197 ave Mhmd V
• Map B5
• 0524 42 55 00

ONCF Railway Station
• Ave Hassan II
• Map B5
• 0890 20 30 40

Gare routière
(coach station)
• Bab Doukkala
• Map G1
• 0524 43 39 33

Most riads and hotels can recommend a car and driver for private hire.

Left **A sensibly dressed tourist** Centre **Tourist brochure** Right **Tourist office**

Top 10 Planning Your Trip

1 Passports & visas

Citizens of the EU, Switzerland, the United States, Canada, Australia and New Zealand need a valid passport to visit Morocco, but no visa. To be able to stay for three months, your passport should be valid for at least six months after your date of arrival. If your time exceeds the three months, then you must get an extension from the central police station *(see p108)*.

2 Insurance

All visitors should take out an insurance policy before travelling to Marrakech. There are no reciprocal health agreements between Morocco and the EU countries, and if you fall ill you will have to pay the doctor's bills. Theft is rare, but it cannot be ruled out.

3 When to go

Marrakech is warm all year round, although January and February see rainfall, with the temperatures dropping during the nights. The summer heat is at its most oppressive and fierce in July and August. The best times to visit are March to June and September to December. The peak tourist season is Easter and Christmas/New Year, so be sure to make reservations well ahead in order to secure a room if you plan to visit during these periods.

4 What to take

Take good, solid footwear as the alleys of the medina are often uneven. Clothes should be light but not revealing. Take something warm for winter evenings. Carry any necessary medication as your own particular brands may not be available. Everything else is easily obtainable in Marrakech at the hyper-market Marjane, on the Route de Casablanca just north of the New City.

5 How long to stay

Marrakech is not exactly a large city and, as such, possesses proportionately few crowd-pulling sights and monuments. Most visitors pass their time sunning themselves on rooftop terraces with frequent forays into the souks. Unless daytrips south to the mountains or to the coastal region of Essaouira are on your agenda, three or four days is long enough.

6 Electricity

The electric current is 220V/50Hz. Moroccan sockets take European-style two-pin plugs, so bring an adaptor.

7 Islamic holidays

The main Islamic holidays follow the lunar calendar. They are Eid El Fitr (29 July in 2014, 18 July in 2015) and Eid El Adha (5 October in 2014, 24 September in 2015). During this time, the city stays shut for two days, so travelling is very difficult. In the holy month of Ramadan (begins 29 June in 2014, 18 June in 2015), many Muslims fast during the day; due to this, most restaurants and eateries are closed until sundown.

8 Tourist office

The Office National Marocain du Tourisme (OMNT; Tel 0524 43 61 31) is a bit inconvenient to reach, located as it is in Place Abdel Moumen Ben Ali in the New City, a taxi ride away from the medina. Moreover, the staff is not particularly well informed. You will find that the staff at your hotel or riad will be of more help.

9 Disabled visitors

Wheelchair users will find Marrakech a tricky place to navigate, especially in the medina where the crowded roads tend to be narrow and in poor condition. Beyond the large hotels and the railway station, very few buildings are disabled-friendly, though the better riads will do their best to accommodate.

10 Language

French and Arabic are the main languages and the signboards are also bilingual. English is spoken by those in the tourism industry.

Local celebrations: Manifesto of Independence Day (11 Jan), May Day (1 May), Feast of the Throne (30 Jul), **see also p106.**

Left **A local *petit taxi*** Centre **Bicycles for hire** Right **A tourist bus does the city rounds**

TOP 10 Getting Around

1 Walking
Walking is usually the best way of getting around Marrakech, since vehicles are not allowed in the narrow alleys of the medina. Expect to get lost frequently, but someone will always help you out.

2 Calèches
These horse-drawn cabs are located on Place Foucault between Jemaa El Fna and the Koutoubia, and by the Bahia Palace and Majorelle Gardens. There are posted fees for typical rides or you can negotiate an hourly rate (90 Dh is reasonable).

3 Taxis
Beige municipal *petits taxis* should be metered, but you may have to prompt the driver to turn it on. The minimum fare is 5 Dh but most trips cost around 10 Dh, with a 50 per cent surcharge at night. Cabs carry a maximum of 3 passengers.

4 Sightseeing Bus Tours
Starting at the tourist office in Place Abdel Moumen Ben Ali, this double-decker, open-topped bus follows two circular routes, taking in the Koutoubia, Place des Ferblantiers (for the Badii and Bahia palaces), the Menara and Majorelle Gardens and Palmeraie. Services are every 30 minutes from 9am to 5pm. The tickets cost 145 Dh (70 Dh for children) and are valid for 24 hours.

5 Bicycles and scooters
Bicycles, scooters and mopeds can be hired at various places, including Bazaar Salah Eddine (off Rue de Bab Agnaou) and along Rue Bani Marine. Hire scooters at Marrakech Motos in Guéliz.

6 To Essaouira
A Supratours bus is the easiest way to get to Essaouira from the city. Buses leave five times a day, starting at 8:30am, from the old train station on Avenue Hassan II in Guéliz. The "Comfort Special" coach service departs at 9:30am. It's wise to book a seat in advance. Or opt for the cheaper, though slightly shabby CTM bus from the *gare routière*. There is also a plane service between Marrakech and Essaouira.

7 Rules of the road
The Moroccan highway code is similar to that of France, so give way on the right (note that whoever is on a town roundabout has priority). Speed limits are 40 or 60 km/h (25 or 37 mph) in city areas, 100 km/h (60 mph) on open roads and 120 km/h (74 mph) on motorways. The road signs are in Arabic and French. As you head south over the Atlas, a 4-wheel-drive is a must for travelling on dirt tracks.

8 Heading over the Atlas
Seats on the buses heading south over the Tizi-n-Tichka and Tizi-n-Test are cheap, but you don't get to stop en route. It is better to hire a car or a *grand taxi*.

9 Car rental
Car hire is quite expensive with local agencies charging around 400 Dh a day. If you need a car only for the drive over the Atlas, a *grand taxi* may be cheaper.

10 *Grands taxis*
Grands taxis are the best way to cross the Atlas – you get to dictate where to stop. Expect to pay from 700 Dh for the whole car on a one-way trip to Ouarzazate.

Car rentals

Avis
• Map B5 • 137 ave Mohammed V • 0524 43 25 25 • www.avis.com

Budget
• Map B4 • 68 blvd Mohammed Zerktouni • 0524 43 11 80 • www.budgetrentacar.com

Europcar
• Map B5 • 63 blvd Mohammed Zerktouni • 0524 43 12 28 • www.europcar.ma

Hertz
• Map B5 • 154 ave Mohammed V • 0524 43 13 94 • www.hertz.com

Supratours: 0524 43 55 25 for national destinations; 0524 43 64 73 for international destinations.

Left **Post office sign** Centre **A Moroccan bank** Right **An ATM**

TOP 10 Useful Information

1 Business and shopping hours

Although a Muslim country, much of Morocco follows a Monday to Friday working week. Business hours for banks are 8:15am–3:45pm Monday to Friday (9:30am–2pm during Ramadan). Shops start their day a bit later but stay open until 8pm or 9pm. On Fridays, the shops in the souks stay shut at lunchtime.

2 Currency

The Moroccan unit of currency is the dirham (Dh), divided into 100 centimes; centimes are of little value but beggars are grateful for them. The most useful coins are the denominations of 1, 2, 5 and 10 dirhams. Try to have a stock of small change with you when travelling by taxi. Notes are in denominations of 20, 50, 100 and 200 dirhams.

3 Banks and ATMs

Banks are clustered on Rue de Bab Agnaou in the medina and Place Abdel Moumen Ben Ali in the New City. Most of the banks have automatic cash dispensers (ATMs), most of which give cash if your card is part of the Cirrus, Maestro or Visa networks. Cash is issued in dirhams only.

4 Credit cards

Credit cards are accepted by most of the high-end hotels. However, this may not be the case for all restaurants in the city. Some places may decline your card in the hope that you will pay cash. Insist that you have no other means of payment and your card may just be accepted.

5 Mobile phones

National operator Maroc-Télécom and rivals Meditél and INWI have arrangements with European networks that allow visitors to use mobiles in Morocco. Calls will, of course, be expensive. If you are visiting for a long period, buy a pre-paid SIM card from either of the operators, with shops just off Place du 16 Novembre in the New City.

6 International phone booths

For overseas calls, use one of the *téléboutiques* (phone offices) dotting the medina, identified by large blue-and-white signs with a telephone handset. The phones take 5 Dh and 10 Dh coins; get change from the person manning the desk. You can use the street cardphones with phonecards from post offices or *tabacs*. The international access code from Morocco is 00.

7 Internet access

There are Internet centres off Jemaa El Fna, but the best one is a spacious, well-equipped centre in Cyber Espace, Arset Moulay Abdesslem (5 Dh per hour).

8 Post offices

The post office on Place du 16 Novembre in Guéliz opens 8am–4:15pm Monday–Friday and 8:30am–noon on Saturday. There is also a post office on the south side of Jemaa El Fna with the same opening times and outside public phones. The railway station post office is open until 6pm on Saturdays. For international express parcels, the Amana Bureau Guéliz is open 8am–6:15pm Monday–Saturday, and there is Chronoposte on Avenue Hassan II. Stamps are also available at tobacconists.

9 Poste restante

The main post office in Marrakech offers a free poste restante service. All mail should bear the first name and surname of the recipient, as well as the post office address. You will need some form of identification when collecting mail.

10 Shipping and couriers

Many shops offer a shipping service for overseas customers; however, it is advisable to take care of the arrangements yourself. The parcel office is next door to the main post office on Place du 16 Novembre.

To call Morocco from abroad, dial 00 212 + number; Marrakech area code is 0524; always dial 10 digits when ringing within the city.

Left **Traditionally dressed women** Centre **Tin Mal Mosque** Right **Photographing the locals**

Top 10 Etiquette

1 Hospitality
For Moroccans, hospitality is more than just tradition; it's a matter of honour. Particularly if you travel out of Marrakech, people you meet may well invite you to their homes to drink tea or have a meal; a refusal could be seen as offensive. Never offer to pay for your meal. Carry a small gift along, like chocolates or cakes.

2 Islam
Islam is a state religion and the king of Morocco is the leader of the faithful. It is therefore considered to be in bad taste to criticise religion. Dress properly *(see below)* and refrain from overt signs of affection. During the fast of Ramadan *(see p103)* do not eat, drink or smoke in public during the day.

3 Dress
Although Moroccan women do wear Western clothes, play it safe and dress conservatively. Headscarves are not necessary but neither women nor men should wear shorts. Women should also avoid mini skirts, baring their midriff or leaving their shoulders bare. Revealing bikini tops should be restricted to the hotel pool.

4 Female travellers
Marrakech is safe for solo female travellers, although you should expect to attract more than your fair share of attention wherever you go. However, avoid travelling down south on your own. People are more conservative south of the Atlas; a woman on her own will draw a lot of unwelcome curiosity.

5 Photographing people
You can take photographs almost anywhere in Morocco but avoid official buildings and anything that looks like it might be police or military. Before turning your camera on anyone, always ask for permission, since the more traditional Moroccans have an ingrained suspicion of any type of image. You may be asked for money by those you photograph, especially in tourist spots and in particular around Jemaa El Fna.

6 Smoking
The stigma of nicotine hasn't yet filtered through to Morocco, and everybody smokes everywhere, all the time. Get used to eating in smoke-filled restaurants and travelling on smoke-filled buses and in smoke-filled taxis.

7 The monarchy
Since the accession of Mohammed VI, attitudes towards the monarchy have relaxed. You may even hear Moroccans criticizing the king's advisors. Even so, the subject of the monarchy is still largely taboo. It is never a good idea to show any disrespect to the king's image, which hangs in shops and in all public places.

8 Tipping
You are expected to tip in restaurants and cafés. As a rule of thumb, leave about 10 per cent unless a service charge is included. You are also expected to tip porters (about 20 Dh is the usual amount) and the staff at your riad – leave 100 Dh on top of the bill.

9 Begging
You may notice that Moroccans give freely to the beggars hanging around the streets, anything from 10 cents to 1 Dh. One of the "Five Pillars of Islam" is charity, which is just as well as there is no social security system to support those unable to work.

10 Visiting mosques
Unlike most other Arab countries, non-Muslims cannot visit mosques or shrines. There are even one or two streets (well marked) in the medina that non-Muslims are not allowed to enter because they lead to holy places. Curiously, this rule was instituted by the French during their protectorate.

Celebrations: Oued Eddahab (14 Aug), King Mohammed VI's Birthday (21 Aug), Green March (6 Nov), Independence Day (18 Nov), **see p103.**

Left **Ain Saiss bottled spring water** Right **Negotiating the Atlas Mountain passes**

TOP 10 Things to Avoid

1 Dehydration
Bottled water is easily available, so be sure to drink lots of it throughout the day. If you don't take in enough liquids, you are likely to end up feeling quite faint or possibly worse.

2 Souk guides
In spite of the strict clampdown on false guides, you may still have people approaching you to offer their services. Always decline. With the help of this book, there's nothing you can't find yourself. Any discount a guide may obtain for you at shops will be negated by his own commission, which the shopkeeper will factor into the price he charges you.

3 Alcohol
Alcohol is frowned upon by Islam. Which is to say that Moroccans drink discreetly and out of the gaze of the general public. Alcohol is forbidden within the medina, given the holy status conferred on it courtesy of its seven shrines. However, hotels and restaurants with a predominantly foreign clientele are allowed some flexibility.

4 Drugs
The country is one of the major producers of cannabis (known locally as *kif*), so drugs are freely available. Ignore all whispered offers of hash around Jemaa El Fna – secret police are present all around, and buying or selling drugs, including hash, is illegal. A fine or, worst case, a prison sentence awaits anyone caught red-handed.

5 Hitchhikers
Hitchhikers dot the road between Marrakech and Ouarzazate. Should you stop to pick them up, your new passenger will invariably attempt to either sell whatever is in his bag or cajole you into detouring off route to a "special" place, that ends up at some friend's or family member's restaurant or shop. It is best not to pick anyone up.

6 Overstretching the plumbing
Even in the best of hotels, Moroccan plumbing is temperamental. Locals use water rather than toilet paper. As a consequence, the pipes may get blocked very quickly if you do use toilet paper. So use it sparingly – older, cheaper hotels even recommend that you dispose of it in the bin provided instead of flushing away the paper.

7 Public displays of affection
Displays of public affection, even walking with arms around each other, are taboo. You will not suffer any extreme form of punishment if caught, but this kind of behaviour is sure to cause offence.

8 Being openly gay
Marrakech has, since the 1970s, been popular with the gay crowd. The city has even been marketed as a gay destination with several riads advertising themselves as gay-friendly. However, homosexuality is forbidden in Morocco and carries a prison sentence. Foreigners are rarely troubled by the police, but it is best to be discreet.

9 Driving Conditions
Always drive with great concentration. Avoid driving in the countryside at night, since bicycles rarely have lights, and there may be animals on the road. In the towns, watch out for motorbikes, which will be coming at you from all sides.

10 Don't believe all you are told
Marrakech inspires the invention of myths. Jimi Hendrix did not write "Castles Made of Sand" after a trip to Essaouira. Sting did not hire out the Amanjena to celebrate his 50th birthday. However, almost everything else you may hear is possibly true. Or possibly not.

Left **An ambulance** Centre **Food stall at Jemaa El Fna** Right **Pharmacy sign**

Top 10 Security and Health

1 Vaccinations and other precautions

No vaccinations are required for visitors entering Morocco, except for those coming from a country where yellow fever exists. However, vaccinations against hepatitis A and B and typhoid are advised. Be sure to pack a small first-aid kit. To prevent sunstroke wear a hat, use a sunblock with a high UV-protection factor and drink lots of water.

2 Personal safety

Violence is rare, though instances of bag snatching and other such opportunistic crimes have been on the rise with the influx of rich foreigners. Be particularly careful when walking through a quiet medina late in the evening. Pickpockets are also common in the souks and on Jemaa El Fna, so be vigilant.

3 Drinking water and food safety

Drink bottled mineral water and freshly squeezed oranges. Don't add ice to your drinks. Avoid street sellers of sweet goods, though the food stalls on Jemaa El Fna are usually safe.

4 Emergencies

In the case of an emergency don't wait for an ambulance: flag a taxi and go to the Polyclinique du Sud in the New City, a private hospital with the best treatment. At all costs, avoid the under-funded public hospitals.

5 Pharmacies

Pharmacies are denoted by a green crescent sign and have well-informed staff, who often speak English. British proprietary drugs may not be available.

6 Doctors and dentists

If the pharmacist cannot help, there are several good doctors and dentists with well-equipped surgeries. All speak French, but a handful also converse in English. Your hotel or riad should have contact details. Otherwise, there is always the Polyclinique du Sud.

7 Animal dangers

Morocco doesn't have particularly harmful insects, but scorpions and snakes are common in the countryside. If you are somewhere in the Atlas Mountains, always check your clothing before getting dressed. Carry some repellent to combat the abundant mosquitoes in desert oasis areas.

8 Serious illness

Being careful about what you eat should prevent any serious illness, but in case of persistent diarrhoea, consult a doctor without delay. Stray dogs may carry rabies and if you are bitten, seek medical attention immediately.

9 Police

In case of problems, try the tourist police first (Brigade Touristique; 0524 38 46 01) at Sidi Mimoun, to the north of Jemaa El Fna (not to be confused with the Judicial Police to the east of Jemaa El Fna). The main police station is on Rue Oued El Makhazine near Jnane El Harti in the New City.

10 Your consulate

Only the French have a consulate in Marrakech. The main UK and US diplomatic offices are in the Moroccan capital, Rabat. In the case of an extreme emergency, there is a Marrakech-based UK honorary consul in the New City.

Directory

Polyclinique du Sud
• Map B4 • 2 rue de Yougoslavie • 0524 44 79 99 • Open 24 hrs

Pharmacie Centrale
• Map B5 • 166 ave Mohammed V, Guéliz • 0524 43 01 58

Pharmacie du Progrès
• Map J3 • Jemaa El Fna • 0524 44 25 63

British Honorary Consul
• Map B4 • 55 blvd Mhmd Zerktouni, Guéliz • 2537 63 33 33

The US Embassy, 0537 63 33 33, and UK Embassy, 0537 76 22 65, are both in Rabat. The US Consulate, 0522 26 45 50, is in Casablanca.

Left **Souk wares** Centre **Dining area** Right **A local serving mint tea**

TOP 10 Shopping and Eating

1 Bargaining

Haggling is de rigueur in the souks. If you don't haggle, you may pay massively over the odds. It all revolves around the considerable difference between the price offered by the seller and the price that he will actually accept if pushed. Shop around and get a few different quotes on identical items before the game begins in earnest.

2 The offer of tea

You will invariably be offered tea as part of the bargaining process. Accepting places you under no obligation to buy. It does, however, allow the seller more time to draw your attention to other potential sales. If you aren't that interested in what he has to offer in the first place, then definitely decline the tea.

3 Avoiding the hard sell

The sales pitches of the souk traders are nothing if not amusing. But if you are not interested then just walk on, don't respond and don't catch anybody's eye. No seller is going to waste time on somebody who is not going to purchase goods.

4 How will it look at home?

A souk is a seductive place with items that may tempt you into a purchase. But stop to consider before you buy: how well will a brass platter the size of a tractor wheel fit with your furniture at home? And would you actually dare to wear the canary-yellow slippers and take a stroll down a high street at home?

5 For something different

If you want a break from the monotony of the always busy souks and wish to purchase something more unique but distinctly Moroccan, visit some of the shops that line the medina, such as Atelier Moro, Kif Kif and Kulchi *(see p70)*, or Scènes du Lin *(see p78)* up in the New City. All these places are run by young designers with a very unique take on local crafts and traditions.

6 Types of Restaurants

There are two types of restaurant in Marrakech: those that offer Moroccan food and those that offer international food. The Moroccan restaurants either feature an à la carte or set menu. The set-menu meal is something you do once and never repeat again *(see below)*. Your next evening's meal could probably be Moroccan à la carte, and if you're around a third night, you may want to dine at one of the restaurants serving excellent international cuisine.

7 The set meal

In the cheaper restaurants a set meal consists of a starter (soup or salad), followed by a main dish and finishing with a dessert (usually something like a crème caramel or fruit). At the more expensive restaurants such a meal involves more courses than could ever be eaten.

8 Opening hours and reservations

Many restaurants open only for dinner, typically from around 7:30pm until 10:30 or 11pm. You may find it difficult to scout a place for lunch away from Jemaa El Fna or the New City. Reservations are advisable for popular restaurants *(see pp52–3)*.

9 Alcoholic drinks

Most restaurants frequented by Western tourists have a license to serve alcohol. The Moroccan rosé wines are perhaps the best of the lot. In Ramadan *(see p103)* some restaurants that normally serve alcohol stop selling it.

10 Prices

It is possible to eat well for not very much. However, many of the more popular and fashionable restaurants in Marrakech charge European prices. The prices given on menus usually include all taxes, but check if the service is included.

The pharmacies are generally open by 8:30am and stay shut for lunch.

Left **Top-end Palmeraie hotel** Centre **Stylish Palais Rhoul** Right **Comfortable rooms at Hotel Pacha**

Top 10 Accommodation Tips

1 Choosing a hotel

Marrakech has an abundance of stylish accommodation, many of which are either riads *(see below)* or *maisons d'hôtes*, a term that roughly translates to mean "boutique hotels". Some of these places are so stunning, you may find it hard to drag yourself into the throng of the medina. However, for those who find comfort in standard international hotels, there are plenty of those too.

2 Riads

A riad is a house in the medina with a courtyard. Uniquely Moroccan, they can range from a cosy four rooms to close to 20, from humble to ultra-stylish. Nearly all are privately-owned guesthouses and the levels of service and luxury tend to reflect the personalities – and financial resources – of their owners. It is possible to rent a whole riad at a reduced rate. Many riads offer transport to and from the airport.

3 Location, location, location

All the riads are in the medina. The closer you are to Jemaa El Fna, the central whirlpool of Marrakech, the better. The big international hotels are in Hivernage, between the medina and the airport – a taxi ride away from all the action. Anyone seeking to get away from it all might consider retreating to a luxury hideaway in the Palmeraie palm grove, to the north of the medina.

4 Classifications

The Moroccan government has an official classification for hotels, with a one- to five-star grading system. This system, however, is not applied to riads. Listed hotels are often ambitiously graded, and it is not recommended that you venture below three stars.

5 Prices

By law, prices for accommodation must be shown in the reception area as well as in rooms. Be aware, however, that these prices rarely include tax and they do not include breakfast. Again, riads and *maisons d'hôtes* are exempted from this rule.

6 Negotiating a lower price

Negotiating a lower price for a hotel room is common – and fruitful. At slack times, it is possible to obtain reductions of up to 30 per cent. It is a waste of time, however, during high season or with most riads.

7 High and low season

High season is Christmas and New Year and the weeks around Easter. At such times, prices of rooms can go up by as much as 25 per cent, and that's if you can find one – you really need to have something booked months in advance. September and October are generally also busy as the worst of the summer heat is over. January and February are low season.

8 Disabled access

Most accommodation in the medina is not wheelchair accessible, as Moroccan houses are built with lots of steps. The international hotels in Hivernage are the best bets, as many of them are disabled-friendly.

9 Travelling with kids

Riads are not great places to holiday with kids. Being essentially small, former family homes with a central courtyard, noise carries to all rooms. Unless your children are remarkably quiet, you are liable to disturb other guests.

10 Meals

All riads and *maisons d'hôtes* offer breakfast. Few have restaurants but all have kitchens, where lunch and dinner can be prepared to order and usually eaten in the courtyard or on the roof terraces. The food from riad kitchens is as good, if not superior, to most of the local restaurants.

Price Categories

For a standard double room per night with taxes and breakfast if included.

Dh	under Dh500
Dh Dh	Dh500–1500
Dh Dh Dh	Dh1500–2500
Dh Dh Dh Dh	Dh2500–3500
Dh Dh Dh Dh Dh	over Dh3500

Left **Le Méridien N'Fis** Right **Swimming pool at Hotel Es Saadi**

TOP 10 International and Chain Hotels

1 Le Méridien N'Fis

A five-minute taxi ride from the medina. It has 277 rooms, restaurants, a popular nightclub and an excellent spa. The architecture is utilitarian but it does have a nice garden setting. *Map C7 • Ave Mohammed VI, Hivernage • 0524 33 94 00 • www.lemeridienhotels.com •* Dh Dh Dh Dh

2 Royal Mirage Marrakech

A former Sheraton property set within its own walled gardens, the rooms are laid out around a vast central garden pool. *Map C7 • Ave de la Menara, Hivernage • 0524 35 10 00 • www.royalmiragehotels.com •* Dh Dh Dh Dh

3 Sofitel Marrakech

The 207-room Sofitel boasts less offensive architecture, brighter rooms and is closer to the medina. What's more, the excellent Comptoir and Table du Marché *(see p79)* are just a minute's walk away. *Map G5 • Rue Harroun Errachid, Hivernage • 0524 42 56 00 • www.sofitel.com •* Dh Dh Dh Dh

4 Les Jardins de la Koutoubia

Steps away from the Koutoubia Mosque, this well-concealed five-star hotel is relatively modern. The rooms are smart and have full facilities. A swimming pool dominates the central courtyard, while the spectacular roof garden has lovely views. *Map J3 • 26 rue de la Koutoubia, Medina • 0524 38 88 00 • www.lesjardinsdelakoutoubia.com •* Dh Dh Dh Dh

5 Club Med La Medina

Located in a vast palm grove in the centre of town, this all-inclusive "village" has 300 bungalows, a pool and a spa that brims with activities, from bridge to flying trapeze. Table tennis and guided mountain-bike rides are also available. *Map J4 • Jemaa El Fna • 0524 42 58 00 • www.clubmed.co.uk •* Dh Dh Dh Dh

6 Hotel Es Saadi

Come here for Moroccan-style luxury. Set in extensive gardens, this hotel offers 150 rooms and 90 suites, plus ten villas with private pool. There is also a luxurious spa *(see p41)*. *Map C6 • Ave El Kadissia, Hivernage • 0524 44 88 11 • www.essaadi.com •* Dh Dh Dh Dh

7 Tichka Salam

Located on the Casablanca road, a 15-minute taxi ride from the medina, the hotel boasts the best pool in town, two restaurants and a bar with interiors by Bill Willis *(see p38)* verging on the ridiculous. Fun, though remote. *Route de Casablanca, Semlalia • 0524 44 87 10 •* Dh Dh Dh

8 Ibis Moussafir

A modern but very standard Ibis hotel, the Moussafir may be a ten-minute taxi ride from the medina, but it has the advantage of being close to the train and Supratours stations on the western edge of Guéliz. *Map B5 • Ave Hassan II, Place de la gare • 0524 43 59 29 • www.ibishotel.com •* Dh Dh

9 Hivernage Hotel and Spa

This is a stylish and modern, 34-room, independently owned hotel. Just outside the medina walls, it has an excellent restaurant in the Table du Marché, a popular patisserie and beautiful spa. *Map G4 • Cnr of ave Echouhada and rue du Temple, Hivernage • 0524 42 41 00 • www.hivernage-hotel.com •* Dh Dh Dh

10 Atlas Asni

The Atlas chain has two hotels in Marrakech and this is the cheaper. Nothing to look at from outside, the 334 rooms, including 28 suites, are pleasant enough and there is a swimming pool and a fitness centre, if you're looking for a workout after sightseeing. Guests can also access the spa facilities of its ritzier sister hotel nearby. *Map B6 • Ave Mohammed VI, Guéliz • 0524 33 99 00 • www.hotelsatlas.com •* Dh Dh Dh

Left **Hotel Ali sign** Centre **Rooms in Hotel Sherazade** Right **Hotel Gallia**

TOP 10 Hostels and Other Cheapies

1 Grand Tazi

A legendary medina hotel that's well past its sell-by date (rooms are worn and battered), it has retained its popularity thanks to its prime location, within sniffing distance of Jemaa El Fna. It has a large swimming pool and a lobby area where alcohol is served. *Map J4 • Cnr of ave El Mouahidine and rue de Bab Agnaou, Medina • 0524 44 27 87 • Dh*

2 Hotel Gallia

Of all the budget options in the by-lanes off Rue Bab Agnaou, this is one of the best, with en-suite rooms arranged around two charming Andalusian-style courtyards. Be sure to book in advance. *Map J4 • 30 rue de la Recette, off rue de Bab Agnaou, Medina • 0524 44 59 13 • www.ilove-marrakesh.com/hotelgallia • Dh*

3 Hotel Medina

On a street full of cheap rooms, the Medina stands out for its cleanliness and the hospitality of the owners. The really impecunious can sleep on the roof terrace for just 30 Dh. Note that the showers are communal. *Map K4 • 1 derb Sidi Bouloukat, Medina • 0524 44 29 97 • Dh*

4 Hotel Souria

A tiny, popular hotel. It's basic and you pay extra (10 Dh) to use the communal showers – shared by the nine rooms. But the place is homely. *Map J4 • 17 rue de la Recette, off rue de Bab Agnaou, Medina • Dh*

5 Djemaa El Fna Hotel Cecil

This hotel offers excellent value for money, given its central location and facilities, which include en-suite rooms, a rooftop terrace and Wi-Fi. Its pleasant interior is finished in Moroccan cedarwood. *Map J3 • Derb Sidi Bouloukate • www.djemaaelfnahotelcecil.com • No credit cards • Dh*

6 Hotel Ali

A popular launch pad for trips to the Atlas, this is one of the busiest budget hotels in town. The rooms are a bit of a mixed bag, so inspect a few prior to booking. Multi-occupancy rooms (up to four people) are available. *Map J4 • Rue Moulay Ismail, Medina • 0524 44 49 79 • www.hotel-ali.com • No credit cards • Dh*

7 Hotel de Foucauld

One of the more salubrious of the budget options; the rooms are clean, have heating and telephones, plus en suites with reliably hot water. There are fine views of the Koutoubia from the roof terrace. *Map J4 • Ave El Mouahidine, Medina • 0524 44 08 06 • Dh Dh*

8 Hotel Sherazade

This hotel offers a wide range of rooms, from mini-apartments to Spartan sweat boxes on the roof. It's very professionally run with a lovely tiled courtyard and an extensive roof terrace with a tent area for dining. Advance booking is essential. *Map K4 • 3 derb Djama, Medina • 0524 42 93 05 • www.hotelsherazade.com • Dh*

9 Hotel Farouk

Owned by the same people as the Hotel Ali, this is one of the best budget options for anyone looking to stay close to the attractions of the New City. Rooms vary greatly, so view several before choosing. All the rooms have en-suite bathrooms. *Map B5 • 66 ave Hassan II, Guéliz • 0524 43 19 89 • Dh*

10 Hotel Toulousain

Right in the heart of the New City, the Toulousain (established by a Frenchman from Toulouse) has been around forever – US Beat writer William Burroughs was a regular here. The rooms surround a leafy courtyard and there are plenty of good cafés and restaurants nearby, including the popular Café du Livre *(see p79)* next door. *Map B5 • Rue Tarek Ben Ziad, Guéliz • 0524 43 00 33 • www.hoteltoulousain.com • Dh*

Price Categories

For a standard double room per night with taxes and breakfast if included.		
	Dh	under Dh500
	DhDh	Dh500–1500
	DhDhDh	Dh1500–2500
	DhDhDhDh	Dh2500–3500
	DhDhDhDhDh	over Dh3500

Left **Hotel Jnane Mogador** Right **Tchaikana**

Top 10 Budget but Chic

1 Tchaikana

Close to the Musée de Marrakech *(see p68)*, this riad has two suites, two big double rooms and one smaller double room. Delphine, one half of the friendly Belgian couple who run the place, is an expert in souk shopping. *Map K2 • 25 derb El Ferrane, Quartier Azbest, Medina • 0524 38 51 50 • www.tchaikana.com* • DhDh

2 Riad Magi

This unpretentious and tasteful riad offers six colourful en-suite rooms overlooking a central courtyard with orange trees and fountains. Breakfast is served on a charming roof terrace to a backdrop of city and mountain views. In-house cookery lessons can be arranged. *Map K3 • 79 derb Moulay Abdel-kader, off derb Dabachi • 0524 42 66 88 • www.riad-magi.com • No credit cards* • DhDh

3 Dar Fakir

A short distance from Jemaa El Fna, Dar Fakir is like a Buddha Bar chill-out lounge, with a cushion-strewn roofed courtyard adorned with artifacts from India, Thailand and Morocco. It has eight chic guest rooms and a roof terrace from which you can hear the crowds on the nearby square. *Map K3 • 16 derb Abou El Fadail, Kenaria, Medina • 0524 44 11 00 • www.darfakir.com* • DhDh

4 Hotel Trésor

Close to the main square, yet out of earshot, is this little gem of a riad. The Italian owner has put his tasteful stamp on the 14 rooms, with collectables, light fittings and artworks that give this airy hotel a boutique feel. *Map J3 • 77 Sidi Boulokat Riad Zitoun Kdim, Jemaa El Fna • http://p52975.typo3server.info • No credit cards* • DhDh

5 Hotel Jnane Mogador

A restored 19th-century residence that falls between a riad and hotel, it has 17 rooms around a central courtyard with a fountain and grand staircase. The decor may lack sophistication, but the place represents excellent value. *Map K4 • 116 rue Riad Zitoun El Kedim, Derb Sidi Bouloukat, Medina • 0524 42 63 23 • www.jnanemogador.com* • Dh

6 Riad Blanc

A group of five riads, well located between Maison Tiskiwine and the Dar Si Said Museum *(see pp62–3)*. It has been lovingly decorated in a traditional style with green-tiled eaves, flesh-toned *tadelakt* walls *(see p36)* and carved stucco. Rooms are small and there's a courtyard plunge pool, a rooftop Jacuzzi and a *hammam*. *Map K4 • 25 derb Si Said, Medina • 0524 38 89 05* • DhDh

7 Riad O2

This stunning place has a terracotta-tiled courtyard. Rooms are a fusion of Moroccan and cool minimalism – with quirky names (the Chewing Gum Room, the Egg Suite). *Map J1 • 97 derb Semmaria, Sidi Ben Slimane • 0524 37 72 27 • www.riado2.com* • DhDh

8 Dar Salam

This riad is more like a Moroccan B&B. Apart from seven bedrooms, it has two tents on the roof: large marquees with showers and toilets. *Map H1 • 162 derb Ben Fayda Arset Hiheri, Rue Legza, Bab Doukkala • 0524 38 41 41 • www.dar-salam.com* • Dh

9 Riad Altair

Close to the 12th-century Bab Doukkala is this sophisticated riad with six elegant rooms. There are views of the Atlas Mountains from the roof terrace. *Map H2 • 21 derb Zaouia, Medina • 0524 38 52 24 • www.riadaltair.com* • DhDhDh

10 Riad Nejma Lounge

The funkiest riad in town, with its striking colours, looks like it's from a Lenny Kravitz video shoot. A plunge pool in the courtyard and a roof terrace add to its "loungey" feel. *Map G1 • 45 derb Sidi M'hamed El Haj, Bab Doukkala • 0524 38 23 41 • www.riadnejmalounge.com* • DhDh

Left **Riad Kaiss** Centre **Dar Attajmil** Right **Roof terrace on Riad Noga**

Top 10 Mid-range Riads

1 Dar Attajmil

A lovely little riad with just four rooms, it is a short meandering walk north of Jemaa El Fna, and convenient for you to drop in at the souks and Mouassine *(see p68)*. It's an intimate place that bears the stamp of its (English-speaking) Italian owner. *Map J3 • 23 rue Laksour, off rue Sidi El Yamami • 0524 42 69 66 • www.darattajmil.com • Dh Dh*

2 Riad 72

This stylish Italian-owned riad is very Milan-meets-Marrakech. The house is traditional but the furniture is all imported. There is one dramatically large main suite and three smaller double rooms, plus a solarium and a *hammam*. *Map H2 • 72 Arset Awsel, Bab Doukkala • 0524 38 76 29 • www.riad72.com • Dh Dh Dh*

3 Riad Zina

If red happens to be your favourite colour, then this funky riad with a 1970s feel is the place for you. The spacious suite can sleep up to five people. *Map J1 • 38 derb Assabane, Riad Larousse • 0524 38 52 42 • Dh Dh*

4 Dar Doukkala

Seven high-ceilinged rooms and suites in this enchanting *maison d'hotes* are filled with wonderful period details, and clawfoot tubs in the bathrooms. Other eccentricities include a wall of lanterns above a small terrace pool. *Map H2 • 83 rue Bab Doukkala, Dar El Bacha • 0524 38 34 44 • Closed for five weeks in summer • www.dardoukkala.com • Dh Dh*

5 Riad Noga

A spacious riad with a homely air and efficient service, it has a pool and all the rooms have TV sets, sound systems and cosy fireplaces. *Map L3 • 78 derb Jdid, Douar Graoua • 0524 38 52 46 • www.riadnoga.com • Dh Dh Dh*

6 Riad Lotus Ambre

The Lotus has four double rooms and one suite which boast branded bed linen, Bang & Olufsen plasma screens and whumping sound systems. Warhol art decorates the walls. If bling's your thing, this riad's for you. *Map J3 • 22 derb Fhal Zefriti, Quartier Leksour • 0524 43 15 37 • www.riadslotus.com • Dh Dh Dh*

7 Riad Azzar

This tasteful, Dutch-owned riad is unique for its small, heated plunge pool right in the middle of the courtyard. Three of the six rooms are suites and come equipped with luxuries such as fireplaces and air conditioning. *Map K3 • 94 derb Moulay Abdelkader, off derb Dabachi • 0661 15 81 79 • www.riadazzar.com • Dh Dh Dh*

8 Riad Hayati

This elegant riad combines Moorish architecture with subtle tones of Arabia, Turkey and Persia, in the form of antique *kilims*, rich Ottoman tapestries and a Damascene fountain – reminders of the years that its British owner spent in the Middle East. *Map L4 • 27 derb Bouderba, off rue Riad Zitoun El Jedid • 0044 (0)7770 431 194 (UK) • www.riadhayati.com • Dh Dh Dh*

9 Riad Kaiss

This riad is everything that you might have imagined a Marrakech riad to be. Pink-walled and green-tiled terraces and crisp, pristine white linen in the bedrooms. Its courtyard is planted with orange and lemon trees. *Map K5 • 65 derb Jedid, off rue Riad Zitoun El Kedim • 0524 44 01 41 • www.riadkaiss.com • Dh Dh Dh*

10 Riad Kniza

A palatial riad filled with *objets d'art*. For 35 years its Moroccan antique dealer/owner has been the quintessential guide to the city, showing around stars such as Tom Cruise and Brad Pitt, and at least one US president. *Map G1 • 34 derb L'Hôtel, Bab Doukkala • 0524 37 69 42 • Closed for some time each summer; phone in advance for details • www.riadkniza.com • Dh Dh Dh*

All riads listed on these pages are located within the medina.

Riyad El Cadi

Price Categories

For a standard double room per night with taxes and breakfast if included.		
	Dh	under Dh500
	DhDh	Dh500–1500
	DhDhDh	Dh1500–2500
	DhDhDhDh	Dh2500–3500
	DhDhDhDhDh	over Dh3500

TOP 10 Mid-range Riads (continued)

1 Talaa 12

A contemporary, eight-room riad, it is decorated in a simple and uncluttered, yet appealing style. The traditional feel that permeates the place is augmented by modern comforts such as air conditioning and a *hammam*. It's located right on the doorstep of the souks. *Map K2 • 12 Talaa Ben Youssef • 0524 42 90 45 • www.talaa12.com* • DhDhDh

2 Riyad El Cadi

A rambling maze of a riad, it is made up of eight connected houses. It's a beautiful place to lose yourself – admiring the collected Islamic art along the way. The staff is super efficient and the quality of service is second to none. *Map K3 • 87 derb Moulay Abdelkader, off derb Dabachi • 0524 37 86 55 • www.riyadel cadi.com* • DhDhDh

3 Riyad Edward

In the remote north of the medina, Edward has a raffish, bohemian charm uniquely its own. A *hammam*, a beautiful garden, pool and a roof terrace are among the many facilities for days of indolent lounging. *Map D4 • 10 derb Maristan • 0524 38 97 97 • www.riyadedward.com* • DhDhDh

4 Riyad Al Moussika

A beautifully restored and maintained former grandee's home, it is especially notable for its good food – including an enormous breakfast of eggs, pancakes, pastries and fruit. *Map K3 • 62 derb Boutouil, Kennaria • 0524 38 90 67 • Closed for Ramadan • www.riyad-al-moussika.com* • DhDhDh

5 Riad El Mezouar

A serene, white-washed riad with large rooms fitted with contemporary furnishings. Its only drawback is the location 15 minutes from Jemaa El Fna. *Map L3 • 28 derb El Hammam • 0524 33 69 60 • www.mezouar.com* • DhDh

6 Riad El Arsat

This riad has ten rooms split between "winter" and "summer" houses at either end of what is the largest garden of any riad in the medina – with a pool and free-roaming tortoises. The decor mixes traditional Moroccan with European Art Deco. *Map L3 • 10 bis, Derb Chemaa, Arset Loughzail • 0524 38 75 67 • www.riad-elarsat-marrakech.com* • DhDhDh

7 Les Jardins de la Medina

It is not hard to see why a 19th-century prince chose this riad for his residence. Set in luxuriant gardens, this boutique establishment has 36 rooms that blend modern amenities with traditional Moroccan splendour. There is also a lovely pool, a *hammam* and a respected cookery school. *Map K7 • 21 derb Chtouka, Quartier Kasbah • 0524 38 18 51 • www.lesjardinsdelamedina.com* • DhDhDh

8 Riad Sindibad

In this seven-room riad, the bedrooms come in a variety of different colours of *tadelakt*. All the rooms are air conditioned and equipped with satellite television. Amenities include a *hammam*, Jacuzzi and solarium. *Map D4 • 413 Arset Ben Brahim, Bab Doukkala • 0524 38 13 10 • www.riadsindibad.com* • DhDh

9 Riad El Ouarda

A beautifully restored 17th-century riad, deep in the heart of the northern medina, well away from the crowds. Each room is differently styled. The roof terrace is one of the best in Marrakech. *Map J1 • 5 derb Taht Sour Lakbir • 0524 38 57 14 • www.riadelouarda.com* • DhDhDh

10 Bab Firdaus

This striking riad is just a few steps from the historic Bahia and Badii palaces *(see pp24–5 and 62)*. The three suites and four guest rooms are all absolutely sumptuous, heavily bedecked with sculpted plaster decoration and carved cedar ceilings. *Map L4 • 57 rue Bahia • 0524 38 00 73* • DhDhDh

Left **Riad El Fenn** Centre **Mamounia** Right **The Royal Mansour**

Top 10 Luxury Riads and Hotels

1 Riad El Fenn

A definite A-list riad comprising 21 fashion-magazine-stylish suites sharing four courtyards, a *hammam*, library, bar and restaurant, three pools and a screening room. ⓢ *Map J3 • Derb Moulay Abdallah Ben Hezzian, Medina • 0524 44 12 10 • www.el-fenn.com* • ⒹⒽⒹⒽⒹⒽⒹⒽ

2 Mamounia

A multimillion-dollar renovation has transformed the Mamounia into the best hotel in North Africa. Smartly dressed non-guests may catch a glimpse of this breathtaking building by frequenting the bar *(see pp28–9)*. ⓢ *Map H5 • Ave Bab Jedid, Medina • 0524 38 86 00 • www.mamounia.com* • ⒹⒽⒹⒽⒹⒽⒹⒽⒹⒽ

3 Riad Farnatchi

Buried deep in the medina, Farnatchi is sheer luxury. It's an all-suite hotel with Philippe Starck fittings and custom-made furniture. It also boasts possibly the best informed, most capable manageress in town. ⓢ *Map K2 • 2 derb Farnatchi, Medina • 0524 38 49 10 • www.riadfarnatchi.com* • ⒹⒽⒹⒽⒹⒽⒹⒽ

4 The Royal Mansour

The last word in luxury lies behind a four-ton bronze door. Sublime service, a library, lounge, spa, bars and a stellar French restaurant all add to the fabulous experience. ⓢ *Map G4 • Rue Abou Abbas El Sebti, Medina • 0524 80 80 80 • www.royalmansour.ma* • ⒹⒽⒹⒽⒹⒽⒹⒽⒹⒽ

5 Villa des Orangers

A grand residence that once belonged to a judge, this boutique hotel has 21 suites arranged around two beautiful courtyards. The roof terrace has unrivalled views of the Koutoubia. ⓢ *Map J5 • 6 rue Sidi Mimoun, Medina • 0524 38 46 38 • www.villadesorangers.com* • ⒹⒽⒹⒽⒹⒽⒹⒽⒹⒽ

6 Riad Enija

Three adjoined houses and a wild garden courtyard make up this striking riad. Rooms verge on the fantastical, with furniture fashioned by international artists. Do you photograph or sleep in the beds? ⓢ *Map K2 • 9 derb Mesfioui, Medina • 0524 44 09 26 • www.riadenija.com* • ⒹⒽⒹⒽⒹⒽⒹⒽ

7 La Sultana

This luxury hotel is discreetly hidden off a court beside the Saadian Tombs. The interiors, a riot of Asian and African styles, are a complete contrast. It's one of the few hotels in the medina with a decent-sized pool (plus spa). ⓢ *Map K6 • 403 rue de la Kasbah, Medina • 0524 38 80 08 • www.lasultanamarrakech.com* • ⒹⒽⒹⒽⒹⒽⒹⒽ

8 Red House

A purpose-built boutique hotel in a traditional style just outside the medina walls. Its rooms are five-star standard with facilities such as minibars and Internet access but the place feels like a private villa, complete with gardens and a pool. ⓢ *Map G3 • Ave El Yarmouk, Hivernage • 0524 43 70 40 • www.theredhouse-marrakech.com* • ⒹⒽⒹⒽⒹⒽ

9 Kssour Agafay

Kssour Agafay is North Africa's first private members' club. Built in the late 15th century, it is a UNESCO World Heritage building. It has been magnificently restored, with six stunning suites on the upper levels usually available to non-members. ⓢ *Map J3 • 52 Sabet Graoua Ksour, Medina • 0524 36 86 00 • www.kssouragafay.com* • ⒹⒽⒹⒽⒹⒽⒹⒽ

10 Dar Rhizlane

A five-star accommodation with personality, this country mansion-styled residence by star architect Charles Boccara is a short taxi ride from the medina. Rooms are luxurious – some even have their own walled gardens. The ultimate private retreat in the heart of the city. ⓢ *Map C6 • Avenue Jnane El Harti, Hivernage • 0524 42 13 03 • www.dar-rhizlane.com* • ⒹⒽⒹⒽⒹⒽⒹⒽ

For more on Charles Boccara, **see p38.**

Palais Rhoul

Price Categories

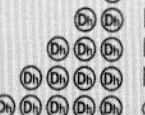

For a standard double room per night with taxes and breakfast if included.

Dh	under Dh500
DhDh	Dh500–1500
DhDhDh	Dh1500–2500
DhDhDhDh	Dh2500–3500
DhDhDhDhDh	over Dh3500

TOP 10 The Palmeraie and Further Afield

1 Jnane Tamsna

This coolest and most elegant of the Palmeraie villas has featured in an array of international fashion magazines but there's plenty of substance here too – surrounding fruit orchards, and vegetable and herb gardens provide the all-organic produce for the kitchen. *Douar Abiad, La Palmeraie • 0524 32 84 84 • www.jnanetamsna.com* • DhDhDhDh

2 Ksar Char Bagh

This maddest of Marrakech accommodations is a virtual re-creation of an Alhambran palace court on a grand scale. At Ksar Char Bagh, it's all about excess – from the heated pool to the cigar salon. The hotel will pick up guests from the airport in reconditioned London taxis. *Djnan Abied, La Palmeraie • 0524 32 92 44 • www.ksarcharbagh.com* • DhDhDhDhDh

3 Les Deux Tours

A landmark piece of architecture by Charles Boccara, this is a beautiful walled retreat of interconnected villas in lush gardens. The softly seductive rooms make lavish use of Boccara's trademark *tadelakt*, not to mention the lawn-fringed pools. *Douar Abiad, La Palmeraie • 0524 32 95 27 • www.les-deuxtours.com* • DhDhDh

4 Dar Zemora

Built in the 1990s as a private villa and set in three acres of gardens, this hotel has just three exquisite suites and three equally fantastic, massive bedrooms. The marble baths are the size of sarcophagi. *Rue El Andalib, La Palmeraie • 0524 32 82 00 • www.darzemora.com* • DhDhDhDh

5 Palmeraie Golf Palace and Resort

This large five-star hotel on the northern edge of the Palmeraie with a golf course attached also has pools, gardens, tennis courts, restaurants and a popular nightclub. *Circuit de la Palmeraie • 0524 36 87 04 • www.pgpmarrakech.com* • DhDhDhDh

6 Palais Rhoul

This hotel's gardens are vast and shared by just 20 rooms. Palais Rhoul has two restaurants and one of the world's best *hammams*. It also runs cookery classes. *Km 5, Dar Tounisi, Route de Fès • 0524 32 94 94 • www.palais-rhoul.com* • DhDhDhDh

7 Caravanserai

A conversion of several village dwellings north of Marrakech, this is the place to hole up and leave modern life behind. The mudbrick architecture is simple but oh-so-chic and there's a beautiful pool, lots of terraces and a *hammam*. A mini-bus shuttles into town twice a day should you wish. *264 Ouled Ben Rahmoune, 40,000 • 0524 30 03 02 • www.hotelcaravanserai.com* • DhDhDh

8 Amanjena

Part of the ultra exclusive Amanresorts group, the place resembles a film set of an Oriental epic. Accommodation consists of 39 private villas, some with their own walled gardens. *Km 12, Route de Ouarzazate • 0524 40 33 53 • www.amanresorts.com* • DhDhDhDhDh

9 Peacock Pavilions

Surrounded by olive groves, this charming and chic boutique guesthouse has six double rooms. Admire the artworks, savour the food or watch a film in the open-air cinema. *Km 13, Route de Ouarzazate, Douar Ladaam • 0664 41 46 53 • www.peacockpavilions.com* • DhDhDh

10 Manzil La Tortue

The tented bedrooms in this rural retreat are set among olive and fruit trees. There are also comfortable villas and a pool with underwater music. Charming hosts and excellent prices. *Km 12, Route de Ouarzazate, Douar Gzoula • 0661 95 55 17 • www.manzil-la-tortue.com* • DhDh

General Index

A

A Year in Marrakech 33
Abu Abdullah Mohammed II 23
Abdel Aziz 62
Abdel Malek 23
Abouzeid, Leila 45
accommodation 110–17
 budget hostels 112
 budget hotels 113
 child-friendly 49
 international and chain hotels 111
 luxury riads and hotels 116
 mid-range riads 114–15
 places to stay 84, 93, 99
 riads 46–7, 110
 tips 110
acrobats 9
activities for children 48–9
Adventures in Morocco 33
Agadir 92
Agdz 97
Agdal Gardens 19, 42
Ahmed, Ba 62
Ahmed El Mansour 21, 24
airlines and airport 102
Aït Benhaddou 96, 99
Aït Ourir 95
Al Badii 78
Al Fassia 52, 79
Alaouites, the 20, 32
alcohol 109 *see also* bars, nightlife, restaurants
Alexander 34–5, 96
Ali Baba and the Forty Thieves 92
Ali Ben Youssef 18
Almohad Mosque 13
Almohads, the 13, 32, 62, 90
Almovarids, the 13, 32, 68
Amanjena 17, 39, 117
Amizmiz 57
Amridil 98
Anti-Atlas, the 92
architecture 36–7
 Mauresque 76
 modern styles 38–9
argan oil 16, 90 *see also* souk souvenirs
Arset el Mamoun see Mamounia Gardens
Arset Moulay Abdesslem 43, 117
art and culture 44–5
Arts in Marrakech Festival (AiM) 44
Asni 56, 89
Association Tameslohte 57
Atelier Moro 70
Atika Chaussures 78
Atlas Asni 111
Atlas Blue 102
Atlas Corporation Studios 95 *see also* films shot in Morocco
Atlas Mountains, the 6, 32, 35, 56–7, 61, 88, 92
 Tizi-n-Test Pass 88–93
 Tizi-n-Tichka Pass 94–9
Au Sanglier Qui Fume 90, 93
auberge
 Souktana 93
 Telouet 99
Avenue Mohammed V 43, 75
Avis 104
Aya's 64

B

Bab Doukkala 18, 61, 78, 81
 Mosque 69
Bab Agnaou 18
Bab Berrima 19
Bab Debbagh 19, 69
Bab El Jdid 45
Bab El Kasbah 91
Bab El Khemis 19
Bab El Rob 18
Bab Firdaus 115
Bab Marrakech 83
Bab Nkob 77
Bab Restaurant 53
babouches (slippers) 14, 16 *see also* souk souvenirs
Bahia Palace 37, 62, 41, 104
Badii Palace 7, **24–5**, 68–9
Bains de Marrakech 40
banks and ATMs 105
Barrage Lalla Takarkoust 56
bars 79, *see also* nightlife
bazaars *see* markets
bargaining (haggling) 109
Bazaar du Sud 70
beaches 83
begging 106
Beldi 17, 70
Belkahia, Farid 45
belly dancing 51, 53, 65
Ben Jelloun, Tahar 45
Ben Youssef Mosque 23, 37, 68
Berbers, the 17, 45, 51, 56–7, 83, 90, 97
Binebine, Mahi 45
Boccara, Charles 39, 76
books on Morocco 33
Boulmane du Dadès 98
Boulangerie El Widad 91
Bowles, Paul 35
British Airways 102
British Honorary Consul 108
British Midland Airways 102
budget accommodation 112–13
budget travel 104
Bureau des guides 91
buses 102
 CTM buses 102
 gare routière (coach station) 102
 over the Atlas 104
 sightseeing bus tours 104
 Supratours 83, 102, 104
 to Essaouira 83, 104
business and shopping hours 105

C

cafés *see also* places to eat, restaurants
Café Arabe 14, 67, 69, 71
Café Atlas 55, 77
Café de France 8
Café des Epices 14, 71
Café du Livre 44, 78, 79
Café Glacier 11, 35
Café les Negociants 77, 79
Grand Café de la Poste 79
Palmeraie d'Or 48
calèches 8, 19, 48, 104
camel
riding 48, 98 *see* Merzouga
trekking 96 *see* Ouarzazate
car rentals 104
Caravanserai 117
Casa Del Mar 84
Cascades d'Ozoud 57
Casino de Marrakech 55
celebrity visitors 34–5
Centre Artisanal 21, 64
Chalet de la Plage 83, 85
Chez Ali 51
Chez Chegrouni 52, 65
Chez Driss 85
Chez Nada 91
Chez Sam 85
children
activities for 48–9
child-friendly accommodation 49
see also riads
Chrob ou Chouf Fountain 23
Church of St Anne *see* Église des Saints-Martyrs de Marrakech
Churchill, Winston 28, 34, 69, 89
Cinéma Eden 63
city walls and gates 7, **18–19**, 45, 61, 69, 77–8, 81, 83, 91, 115
Club Med La Medina 111
coaches *see* buses
Comptoir 53–4, 77, 79, 111
consulates 107
Coralia Club Palmeriva 49
Cordonnerie Errafia 64
Côté Plage 85
country markets 57, 89, 95
credit cards 105
currency 105
cycling 49, 104

D

Dadès Gorge 98
Damgaard, Dane Frederik 83
danger from animals 108
Dar Adul 84
Dar Ahlam 99
Dar Attajmil 47, 114
Dar Bellarj 23
Dar Cherifa 37, 44, 67, 69
Dar Daif 99
Dar Doukkala 114
Dar El Bacha 37, 69
Dar El Bahar 84
Dar El Hajar 13
Dar El Haoura 19
see also fortresses
Dar Fakir 113
Dar Les Cigognes 39
Dar Loulema 84
Dar Moha 52, 71
Dar Rhizlane 116
Dar Salam 113
Dar Si Said Museum 62–3
Dar Yacout 39, 53, 71
Date Festival 98
day trips 56–7
Essaouira 80–85
Tizi-n-Test Pass 88–93
Tizi-n-Tichka Pass 94–9
Days of Glory 76
de Gaulle, General Charles 35
Debbouze, Jamel 45
dehydration 109
desert 97–8
dialling codes 105
Dinanderie 64
disabled access 103, 110
Djemaa El Fna Hotel Cecil 112
doctors 108
dress code 106
drinks
alcohol 109
dehydration 107
getting drunk 107
mint tea 51
see also offer of tea
orange-juice stalls 8
water safety 108
water sellers 9
driving 104
car rentals 104
over the Atlas 107
rules of the road 104
drugs 107

E

Église des Saints-Martyrs de Marrakech (Church of St Anne) 75, 77
electricity 103
El Kelaa M'Gouna 98
emergencies 108
Ensemble Artisanal 70, 77
entertainers **8–11**
entertainment 51
Erfoud 98
Erg Chebbi dunes 98
Essaouira 80–85, 103–4
places to stay 84
places to eat 85
etiquette 106
hammam 40
Night Market, the 10
Europcar 104

F

famous guests *see* celebrity visitors
famous Moroccans 45
fanous (lanterns) 16 *see also* souk souvenirs

Farrell, Colin 34
Fedal, Moha 52
female travellers 106
Ferdaous 85
festivals
Arts in Marrakech Festival (AiM) 44
Date Festival 98
Festivals in Essaouira 44
Horse and Camel Fantasia 44, 97
Marrakech International Film Festival 24, 44
Marrakech Festival of Popular Arts 44
films shot in Morocco 22, 35, 67
Aït Benhaddaou 96
Atlas Corporation Studio 83
Essaouira 80–83
fondouks 14, 67
food 108
fortresses
Dar El Hajar 13
Dar El Haoura 19
fortune tellers 9
fountains 37
Chrob ou Chouf 23
Mouassine 67

G

galleries
Galerie 127 44
Galerie Birkmeyer 78
Galerie Damgaard 83
Galerie Love 27
Galerie Rê 44
Ministerio del Gusto 69
gardens *see* parks and gardens
gare routière (bus station) 102
Gazelle d'Or 93
Getty Jr, John Paul 35
Talitha 35
Gnawa musicians 11, 44, 51–2, 65, 85 *see also* art and culture
golf 49, 117
gorges
Dadès 92
Todra 98
Oued el-Abid 57
Goulmina 98
Grand Café de la Poste 79
Grand Tazi 55, 112
Guéliz 49, 74, 76, 104

H

Haggag, Hassan 45
haggling *see* bargaining
Hakmoun, Hassan 45
Hammam El Bacha 40
Hammam Ziani 41
hammams and spas 40–41, 49
health 108
henna painting 11
herbalists 9
Hertz 104
Hideous Kinky 22, 33, 35, 67
hippy Marrakech 76, 82
historic buildings 37
historic events 32–3
hitchhikers 107
Hivernage 77
Hotel and Spa 41, 111
homosexuality 107
Horse and Camel Fantasias 44, 97
horse riding 48–9
hospitals *see* emergencies
hostels 112
hotels 111–17 *see also* accommodation, places to stay, riads
Hotel Ali 112
Hotel de Foucauld 112
Hotel Es Saadi 41, 51, 76, 111
Hotel Farouk 112
Hotel Gallia 112
Hotel Idou Tiznit 93
Hotel Jnane Mogador 113
Hotel Kenzi Belere 99
Hotel La Kasbah 99
hotels (cont.)
Hotel Les Amandiers 93
Hotel Medina 112
Hotel Palais Salam 91, 93
Hotel Sherazade 112
Hotel Souria 112
Hotel Taroudant 93
Hotel Trésor 113
locations 110
Toulousain 76, 112
hospitality 106
hygiene 10, 108

I

Ibis Moussafir 111
Igherm 92
Ijoujak 90
Imlil 89, 91
In Morocco 33
insurance 103
international and chain hotels 111
Internet 105
Irocha 99
Islam 106
Islamic Art Museum 27, 43, 76
Islamic holidays 103

J

Jamade 64, 69
Jbel (mountain)
Aoulime 92
Guéliz 75
Siroua 92
Toubkal 56, 89
Zagora 97
Jemaa El Fna 6, **8–11**, 48, 52, 69, 104, 112–14, 116
Jemaa El Fna and The Kasbah 60–65
places to eat 65
places to shop 64
Jelloun, Tahar Ben 45
Jet4You 102
jews
mellah (Essaouira) 82, (Marrakech) 62
Miâara Jewish Cemetery 62

Jnane El Harti 43, 48, 76
Jnane Tamsna 39, 117
Joutia 82

K

kasbahs *see also* Jemaa El Fna and the Kasbah
Aït Benhaddou 96, 99
Aït Ben Moro 99
Amerhidil 98
des Juifs 97
du Toubkal 56, 93
Lamrani 99
Mosque 21, 61
Talaat-n-Yacoub 90
Tamadot 89, 93
Tamtattouchte 98
Taourirt 95
Telouet 37, 57, 96
Tiffoultoute 95
Timiderte 97
Tioute 92
Xaluca 99
Kasbah Mosque 21, 61
Kawkab Jeu 48
Kechmara 55, 79
Kenza Melehi 78
Kif Kif 70
Kingdom of Heaven 82, 97
kings *see* sultans and kings
kissaria, The 68, 70
Koubba El Badiyin 68
Koubba Lalla Zohra 13
Koutoubia
Gardens 13, 43
Mosque 6, **12–13**, 23, 53, 61, 65, 75, 90, 104, 111–12, 116
Kozybar 54, 65
Ksar Char Bagh 117
Kssour Agafay 45, 116
ksours (fortified villages)
Goulmina 98
Tamnougalt 97

L

L'Art du Bain 70
L'Avenue 53
L'Heure Bleue 84
L'Orientaliste 78
La Maison Arabe 40, 46, 71
La Maison du Kaftan Marocain 70
La Sultana 40
La Trattoria de Giancarlo 79
Lalla Mira 84
language 49, 103
Lawrence of Arabia 96
Le Berbère Palace 99
Le Cadeau Berbère 64
Le Catanzaro 49
Le Foundouk 23, 39, 52, 71
Le Marrakchi 65
Le Méridien N'Fis 34, 111
Le Palais Oumensour 93
Le Pavillon 71
Le Tanjia 65
Le Tobsil 52, 71
Led Zeppelin 35
Les Alizés Mogador 85
Les Deux Tours 39, 117
Les Jardins de la Medina 115
Les Jardins de la Koutoubia 111
Les Prémises 65
Lord of the Atlas 33
luxury retreats 116

M

Majorelle
blue 27, 43, 47
Gardens 7, **26–7,** 43, 77, 104
Jacques 26, 34, 45
Louis 26
majoun see drugs
Mamounia Hotel 7, **28–9**, 41, 42, 53, 116
Gardens (*Arset el Mamoun*) 29, 42
Manzil La Tortue 117
marathons 49
Marché Central 75, 77–8
Marché Couvert 63–4
markets
Bazaar du Sud 70
Bazaar Salah Eddine 104
country markets 57, 88, 95
Marché Central 75, 77–8
Marché Couvert 63–4
morning market 21
Night Market, the 6, **10–11**
Marrakchi, Leila 45
Marrakech International Film Festival 25, 44
Marrakech Plaza 75
Marjane 103
master musicians of Jajouka 45
Mauresque architecture 75
McDonald's 49, 77
medina
Essaouira 83
Marrakech 62
Medersa Ben Youssef 7, **22–3**, 68
mellah
Essaouira 82
Marrakech 62
Mellah market *see* Marché Couvert
Menara Gardens 42
Merenids, the 20, 32
Merzouga 98
M'Hamid 97
Miâara Jewish Cemetery 62
Miloud El Jouli 70
Ministerio del Gusto 69
mint tea 51 *see also* offer of tea
modern Moroccan styles 38–9
Mohammed V 33
Mohammed VI 33, 44, 62
Mohammed IV 42
morning market 21
Moroccan cuisine 50–51
mosques
Ben Youssef 23, 37, 68
Bab Doukkala 69

mosques (cont.)
Kasbah 21, 61
Koutoubia **12–13**, 23, 53, 61, 65, 75, 90, 104, 111–12, 116
Mouassine 67
Tamegroute 97
Tin Mal 37, 56, 88
visiting 106
Mouassine
Fountain 67, 70, 114
Mosque 67
Moulay Abdellah 22
Moulay Brahim 89
Moulay Hassan 32, 96
Moulay Ismail 32
Mouyal, Elie 45
mountain passes
Tizi-n-Test 88–93
Tizi-n-Tichka 94–9
mud-hut chic 38
Musée de Marrakech 68, 113
Musée des Arts et Traditions Populaires 83
museums
Dar Si Said Museum 68
Islamic Art Museum 27, 43, 76
Musée des Arts et Traditions Populaires 83
Musée de Marrakech 68
Mustapha Blaoui 64, 69, 70
Mutti, Lucrezia 47

N

Narwarma 65
New City, The 43, 44, 74–9, 104
places to shop 78
restaurants, cafés and bars 79
nightlife 44–5, 52–5, 65, 71, 79, 85
Night Market, the 6, **10–11**
Nikki Beach 55

O

Oasiria 49
offer of tea 109
Office National Marocain du Tourisme 103
opening hours 109
orange-juice stalls 8
organized tours 102
Orwell, George 34, 77
Ouarzazate 56, 96, 98–9
river 96
Oued el-Abid 57
Oued Nifis River 90
Ouikadem 56
Ouirgane 90
Ourika Valley 57
outdoor activities 49

P

P. Diddy 34
Pacha 54
palaces
Bahia Palace 37, 41, 62, 104
Badii Palace **24–5**, 68
Palais Rhoul 40, 117
Palazzo Desdemona 84
Palmeraie
Golf Palace 48, 117
gardens 42
hideaways 117
palm groves
Palmery 42
Tafiltalt 98
Ziz 98
parks and gardens 13, **26–7**, 29, 42–3, 48, 69, 76–7, 104
passports and visas 103
Pâtisserie des Princes 65
Peacock Pavilions 117
personal safety 108
pharmacies 108
Pharmacie Centrale 108
Pharmacie du Progrès 108
Polyclinique du Sud 108
phones 105
international phone booths 105
mobile phones 105
photographing people 106
pisé 18, 37–8
Pizzeria Venezia 12, 65
Place
Abdel Moumen Ben Ali 54, 75, 76
de la Liberté 75
des Ferblantiers 25, 63–4
du 16 Novembre 75, 77
du Foucault 10
El Alaouyine 91
Moulay Hassan 81, 83–4
Orson Welles 82
Sour Souika 57
places to eat 65, 71, 85
see also restaurants
places to stay 84, 93, 99 *see also* accommodation, hostels, hotels, riads
places to shop 64, 70, 78
see also souks
Place Vendome 78
plumbing 107
police 108
pony rides 48
port, The (Essaouira) 81
fish stalls 85
post offices 105
poste restante 105
precautions 108
Prince Moulay Mamoun 42
Prince of Persia: The Sands of Time 35
public displays of affection 107

R

Rahba Kedima 15
Ramadan 50, 103
ramparts (Essaouira) 81
Red House 116
Relais du Lac 56
Renaissance 76
Restaurant El Minzah 85
Restaurant Le Jacaranda 79
restaurants 52–3
Essaouira 85

restaurants (cont.)
Jemaa El Fna and the Kasbah 65
New City, The 79
Souks, The 71
riads 46–7, 110
luxury riads 116
mid-range 114–15
Riad 72 114
Riad Al Medina 84
Riad Altair 113
Riad Azzar 114
Riad Blanc 113
Riad des Mers 71
Riad El Arsat 115
Riad El Fenn 46, 116
Riad El Mezouar 115
Riad Enija 39, 46, 116
Riad Farnatchi 46, 116
see also modern Moroccan styles
Riad Hayati 114
Riad Kaiss 39, 47, 114
see also modern Moroccan styles
Riad Kniza 114
Riad Lotus Ambre 114
Riad Nejma Lounge 113
Riad Noga 114
Riad O2 113
Riad Quadra 115
Riad Sindibad 115
Riad Zina 114
Riyad Al Moussika 47, 115
Riyad Edward 115
Riyad El Cadi 46, 115
Riad Tamsna 62–3
Rissani 98
road rules 104
Rolling Stones, The 34, 76
Rôtisserie de la Paix 79
Royal Air Maroc 102
Royal Mansour 116
Royal Mirage Marrakech 111
royalty *see* sultans and kings
Rue de Bab Agnaou 61
Rue de Kasbah 21
Rue du Souk des Fassis 23
Rue Semarine 14
Rue Riad Zitoun El Jedid 62, 64
Rue Riad Zitoun El Kedim 61

S

Saadian dynasty 33
Tombs 7, **20–21**, 41, 61, 64
Gates 91
Sahara 6, 32, 90, 96–8
Saint-Laurent, Yves 7, 27, 34, 42, 76
sand dunes
Erg Chebbi 98
Tinfou 97
Scènes du Lin 78
security 108
set meals 51, 107
seven saints of Marrakech 68
shipping and courier 105
shopping 109
Jemaa El Fna and the Kasbah 65
New City, The 79
Souks, The **14–15**, 66–71, 82
souvenirs **16–17**
see also souks
shopping and dining 109
shrines
Moulay Brahim 89
Sidi Bel Abbas 68
Sidi Mohammed Kebir 89
Sidi Ifni 92
Silvestro 85
Skala du Porte 81
de la Ville 82
ski resorts 57
Skoura 98
smoking 106
snake charmers 8
So 55
Sofitel Marrakech 111
Souks, The 6, **14–15**, 66–71
in Essaouira 82
places to eat 71
places to shop 70
Souk Arabe 91
Souk Berbère 91
Souk des Ferroniers 15
Souk des Babouches 14, 68
Souk des Tapis 15
Souk des Tienturiers 15, 68
Souk El Bab Salaam 15, 64
Souk El Kebir 14, 68
Souk El Khemis 15
Souk Jedid 82
Souk Kimakhine 70
souk guides 107 *see also* bargaining
souvenirs **16–17**
Sous Massa National Park 92
Spanish Quarter 76
sports 49, 96
storytellers 11
sultans and kings
Abdel Aziz 62
Abdel Malek 23
Ahmed El Mansour 21, 24
Ali Ben Youssef 23
Moulay Abdellah 22
Moulay Ismail 32
Moulay Hassan 32, 96
Mohammed IV 42
Mohammed V 33
Mohammed VI 33, 44
Thami El Glaoui 33, 69, 96
Yacoub El Mansour 18
Supratours 80, 104
swimming 49
Barrage Lalla Takarkoust 56
beaches 82
Coralia Club Palmariva 49

T

Table du Marché 111
Taddert 95
tadelakt 36, 38–9
Tafilalt 98
Tafraoute 92
Tahanaoute 89
Talaa 12 115
Taliouine 92
Tamegroute Mosque 97
Tameslohte 57
Tamnougalt 97
Tangier Diaries, The 33
Tanneries, the 68
Tansift Gardens 48
Taros 83, 85
Taroudant 91, 92, 93
taxis
  airport taxis 102
  grands taxis 88, 94, 102, 104
  petits taxis 104
Tazenakht 92
Tchaikana 46, 113
tennis 49
Terrasses de l'Alhambra 8, 10, 65
Thami El Glaoui 32, 69, 96
  see also sultans and kings
The Man Who Knew Too Much 29, 35
The Royal Mansour 116
Théâtre Royal 39, 45, 76
Théatro 55
things to avoid 107
Tichka Hotel 39
Tichka Plateau 91
Tichka Salam 111
Tinfou 97
Tin Mal 57, 90
  Mosque 37, 56, 88
Tinerhir 98
tipping 106
Tizi-n-Test Pass 88–93, 95
  places to stay 93
  West to the Coast 92
Tizi-n-Tichka Pass 94–9
  places to stay 99
  Valley of the Kasbahs 98
Tiznit 92, 93
Todra Gorge 98
tombs
  Koubba El Badiyin 39, 68
  Koubba El Khamsiniya 25
  Koubba Lalla Zohra 13
  Tomb of Yousef Ben Tachfine 13
  Saadian Tombs 7, **20–21**, 41, 61, 64
Toundoute 98
tourist office 103
tours
  bus tours 104
  organised tours 102
  over the Atlas 104
trains 102
Travels of Ibn Battuta 33
Treaty of Tangier 33
tribes
  Alaouites, the 20, 32
  Almohads, the 13, 32, 62, 90
  Almovarids, the 13, 18, 32, 68
  Berbers, the 17, 45, 51, 56–7, 83, 90, 97
  Goundafi 90
  Merenids, the 20, 32
  Ouaouzgite 92
  Saadians, the **20–21**, 32

U

Ultimo Bacio 79

V

vaccinations 108
Villa des Orangers 116
Villa Maroc 84
villages and towns
  Agadir 92
  Asni 89
  Amridil 98
  El Kelaa M'Gouna 98
villages and towns (cont.)
  Ijoujak 90
  Imlil 89
  Ouirgane 89
  Sidi Ifni 92
  Skoura 98
  Tafraoute 92
  Tahanaoute 89
  Taliouine 92
  Tazenakht 92
  Tin Mal 89
  Tinerhir 98
  Tiznit 92
  Toundoute 98
ville nouvelle see New City, The
Viola, Lucien 44
visas *see* passports and visas
visiting mosques 106

W

Wadi Massa 92
walks 63, 69, 77, 91, 97, 104
water 108
  water safety 108
  water sellers 9
when to visit 103
Willis, Bill 38

Y

Yacoub El Mansour 18
Yahya 78
Yousef Ben Tachfine 12
Youssef, Moulay 64

Z

Zagora 97
zellij 36–8
Ziz 98
Zohra, Lalla 13

Acknowledgements

The Author
Andrew Humphreys is a London-based journalist and writer with a particular passion for the Middle East and North Africa. He has written extensively on Morocco for a variety of newspapers, magazines and publishing companies, and is a frequent visitor to Marrakech.

Main Photographer
Alan Keohane has lived in Morocco since 1993 and is the author of the photographic books 'Berbers of Morocco' and 'Bedouin, Nomads of the Desert'. His pictures have appeared in publications such as the New York Times, Marie Claire and Condé Nast Traveller, as well as several other DK Eyewitness Guides. He would like to thank Najat Bouhrim and Naima Sabik for all their help.

Additional Photography
Rough Guides/Roger Norum, Rough Guides/Suzanne Porter

Maps
JP Map Graphics

Arabic Phrase Book
Lexus Ltd

Fact checkers
Majda El Bekhti, Alan Keohane

AT DORLING KINDERSLEY

Publisher
Douglas Amrine

Publishing Manager
Scarlett O'Hara

Managing Art Editor
Mabel Chan

Project Editor
Alastair Laing

Project Designer
Shahid Mahmood

Senior Cartographic Editor
Casper Morris

DTP Operator
Natasha Lu

Production
Anna Wilson, Sophie Argyris

Revisions Team
Emma Anacootee, Caroline Elliker, Anna Freiberger, Rhiannon Furbear, Bharti Karakoti, Sumita Khatwani, Priya Kukadia, Maite Lantaron, Carly Madden, Nicola Malone, Alison McGill, Sam Merrell, Claire Naylor, Erin Richards, Lucy Richards, Sands Publishing Solutions, Susan Searight, Safia Shah

Picture Credits
a - above; b - below/bottom; c - centre; f - far; l - left; r - right; t - top.

The photographer, author and publisher would like to thank the following for their cooperation:

ALAMY IMAGES: Art Kowalsky 30-31; LH Images 75tl; Image State/Royalty Free 35r, mediacolor's 45tl, Nick Hanna 27tl, Photo12 34tr, Realimage 102tr; AL BADII GALLERY: 78tr; L'AVENUE RESTAURANT: 52tl; CHURCHILL HERITAGE LIMITED: 34tl; CORBIS: Bettmann 35tl, Hulton-Deutsch Collection 33bl, Jean-Pierre Lescourret 58-59, John Springer Collection 29bl, Stephane Cardinale 34bl and 44bl; DAR ATTAJMIL: 47tl, 114tl; DK IMAGES: Judith Miller/Lights Camera Action 29cr; LA GAZELLE D'OR: 92tl; GETTY IMAGES: Gallo Images/Shaen Adey 9cr, Andrew Gunners 3bl, Dmitri Kessel 32t, Neil Emmerson 2tc; JARDIN MAJORELLE: 27tr; KASBAH DU TOUBKAL: 56bl; LA MAMOUNIA: 116tc; PALAIS RHOUL: 38tr, 40br, 117tl; RIAD EL-FENN: 46bl, 116tl; RIYAD EL CADI: 46tl, 115tl; TCHAIKANA: 46tl, 113tc; VILLA MAROC: 84tl.

For further information see: www.dkimages.com

Phrase Book: French

In Emergency

Help!	**Au secours!**	*oh sekoor*
Stop!	**Arrêtez!**	*aret-ay*
Call a doctor!	**Appelez un médecin!**	*apuh-lay uñ medsañ*
Call an ambulance!	**Appelez une ambulance!**	*apuh-lay oon oñboo-loñs*
Call the police!	**Appelez la police!**	*apuh-lay lah poh-lees*
Call the fire brigade!	**Appelez les pompiers!**	*apuh-lay leh poñ-peeyay*

Communication Essentials

Yes/No	**Oui/Non**	*wee/noñ*
Please	**S'il vous plaît**	*seel voo play*
Thank you	**Merci**	*mer-see*
Excuse me	**Excusez-moi**	*exkoo-zay mwah*
Hello	**Bonjour**	*boñzhoor*
Goodbye	**Au revoir**	*oh ruh-vwar*
Good night	**Bonsoir**	*boñ-swar*
What?	**Quel, quelle?**	*kel, kel*
When?	**Quand?**	*koñ*
Why?	**Pourquoi?**	*poor-kwah*
Where?	**Où?**	*oo*

Useful Phrases

How are you?	**Comment allez-vous?**	*kom-moñ talay voo*
Very well,	**Très bien**	*treh byañ*
Pleased to meet you.	**Enchanté de faire votre connaissance.**	*oñshoñ-tay duh fehr votr kon-ay-sans*
Where is/are…?	**Où est/sont…?**	*oo ay/soñ*
Which way to…?	**Quelle est la direction pour…?**	*kel ay lah deer-ek-syoñ poor*
Do you speak English?	**Parlez-vous anglais?**	*par-lay voo oñg-lay*
I don't understand.	**Je ne comprends pas.**	*zhuh nuh kom-proñ pah*
I'm sorry.	**Excusez-moi.**	*exkoo-zay mwah*

Useful Words

big	**grand**	*groñ*
small	**petit**	*puh-tee*
hot	**chaud**	*show*
cold	**froid**	*frwah*
good	**bon**	*boñ*
bad	**mauvais**	*moh-veh*
open	**ouvert**	*oo-ver*
closed	**fermé**	*fer-meh*
left	**gauche**	*gohsh*
right	**droite**	*drwaht*
entrance	**l'entrée**	*l'on-tray*
exit	**la sortie**	*sor-tee*
toilet	**les toilettes**	*twah-let*

Shopping

How much does this cost?	**C'est combien s'il vous plaît?**	*say kom-byañ seel voo play*
I would like …	**Je voudrais…**	*zhuh voo-dray*
Do you have?	**Est-ce que vous avez?**	*es-kuh voo zavay*
Do you take credit cards?	**Est-ce que vous acceptez les cartes de crédit?**	*es-kuh voo zaksept-ay leh kart duh kreh-dee*
What time do you open?	**A quelle heure vous êtes ouvert?**	*ah kel urr voo zet oo-ver*
What time do you close?	**A quelle heure vous êtes fermé?**	*ah kel urr voo zet fer-may*
This one.	**Celui-ci.**	*suhl-wee-see*
That one.	**Celui-là.**	*suhl-wee-lah*
expensive	**cher**	*shehr*
cheap	**pas cher, bon marché**	*pah shehr, boñ mar-shay*
size, clothes	**la taille**	*tye*
size, shoes	**la pointure**	*pwañ-tur*
white	**blanc**	*bloñ*
black	**noir**	*nwahr*
red	**rouge**	*roozh*
yellow	**jaune**	*zhohwn*
green	**vert**	*vehr*
blue	**bleu**	*bluh*

Types of Shop

antique shop	**le magasin d'antiquités**	*maga-zañ d'oñteekee-tay*
bakery	**la boulangerie**	*booloñ-zhuree*
bank	**la banque**	*boñk*
bookshop	**la librairie**	*lee-brehree*
cake shop	**la pâtisserie**	*patee-sree*
cheese shop	**la fromagerie**	*fromazh-ree*
chemist	**la pharmacie**	*farmah-see*
department store	**le grand magasin**	*groñ maga-zañ*
delicatessen	**la charcuterie**	*sharkoot-ree*
gift shop	**le magasin de cadeaux**	*maga-zañ duh kadoh*
greengrocer	**le marchand de légumes**	*mar-shoñ duh lay-goom*
grocery	**l'alimentation**	*alee-moñta-syoñ*
market	**le marché**	*marsh-ay*
newsagent	**le magasin de journaux**	*maga-zañ duh zhoor-no*
post office	**la poste, le bureau de poste, le PTT**	*pohst, booroh duh pohst, peh-teh-teh*
supermarket	**le supermarché**	*soo pehr-marshay*
tobacconist	**le tabac**	*tabah*
travel agent	**l'agence de voyages**	*l'azhoñs duh vwayazh*

Sightseeing

art gallery	**la galerie d'art**	*galer-ree dart*
bus station	**la gare routière**	*gahr roo-tee-yehr*
church	**l'église**	*l'aygleez*
garden	**le jardin**	*zhar-dañ*
library	**la bibliothèque**	*beebleeo-tek*
mosque	**la mosquée**	*mos-qay*
museum	**le musée**	*moo-zay*
railway station	**la gare**	*gahr*
tourist information office	**renseignements touristiques, le syndicat d'initiative**	*roñsayn-moñ toorees-teek, sandee-ka d'eenee-syateev*

Staying in a Hotel

Do you have a vacant room?	**Est-ce que vous avez une chambre?**	*es-kuh voo-zavay oon shambr*
double room,	**la chambre à deux**	*shambr ah duh*

with double bed	**personnes, avec un grand lit**	*pehr-son avek un gronñ lee*
twin room	**la chambre à deux lits**	*shambr ah duh lee*
single room	**la chambre à une personne**	*shambr ah oon pehr-son*
room with a bath, shower	**la chambre avec salle de bains, une douche**	*shambr avek sal duh bañ, oon doosh*
I have a reservation.	**J'ai fait une réservation.**	*zhay fay oon rayzehrva-syoñ*

Eating Out

Have you got a table?	**Avez-vous une table libre?**	*avay-voo oon tahbl duh leebr*
I want to reserve a table.	**Je voudrais réserver une table.**	*zhuh voo-dray rayzehr-vay oon tahbl*
The bill please.	**L'addition s'il vous plaît.**	*l'adee-syoñ seel voo play*
I am a vegetarian.	**Je suis végétarien.**	*zhuh swee vezhay-tehryañ*
waitress/ waiter	**Madame, Mademoiselle/ Monsieur**	*mah-dam, mah-demwahzel/ muh-syuh*
menu	**le menu, la carte**	*men-oo, kart*
fixed-price menu	**le menu à prix fixe**	*men-oo ah pree feeks*
cover charge	**le couvert**	*koo-vehr*
wine list	**la carte des vins**	*kart-deh vañ*
glass	**le verre**	*vehr*
bottle	**la bouteille**	*boo-tay*
knife	**le couteau**	*koo-toh*
fork	**la fourchette**	*for-shet*
spoon	**la cuillère**	*kwee-yehr*
breakfast	**le petit déjeuner**	*puh-tee deh-zhuh-nay*
lunch	**le déjeuner**	*deh-zhuh-nay*
dinner	**le dîner**	*dee-nay*
main course	**le plat principal**	*plah prañsee-pal*
starter, first course	**l'entrée, le hors d'oeuvre**	*l'oñ-tray, or-duhvr*
dish of the day	**le plat du jour**	*plah doo zhoor*
café	**le café**	*ka-fay*

Menu Decoder

baked	**cuit au four**	*kweet oh foor*
beef	**le boeuf**	*buhf*
beer	**la bière**	*bee-yehr*
boiled	**bouilli**	*boo-yee*
bread	**le pain**	*pan*
butter	**le beurre**	*burr*
cake	**le gâteau**	*gah-toh*
cheese	**le fromage**	*from-azh*
chicken	**le poulet**	*poo-lay*
chips	**les frites**	*freet*
chocolate	**le chocolat**	*shoko-lah*
coffee	**le café**	*kah-fay*
dessert	**le dessert**	*deh-ser*
egg	**l'oeuf**	*l'uf*
fish	**le poisson**	*pwah-ssoñ*
fresh fruit	**le fruit frais**	*frwee freh*
garlic	**l'ail**	*l'eye*
grilled	**grillé**	*gree-yay*
ham	**le jambon**	*zhoñ-boñ*
ice, ice cream	**la glace**	*glas*
lamb	**l'agneau**	*l'anyoh*
lemon	**le citron**	*see-troñ*
meat	**la viande**	*vee-yand*
milk	**le lait**	*leh*
mineral water	**l'eau minérale**	*l'oh meeney-ral*
oil	**l'huile**	*l'weel*
onions	**les oignons**	*leh zonyoñ*
fresh orange juice	**l'orange pressée**	*l'oroñzh presseh*
fresh lemon juice	**le citron pressé**	*see-troñ presseh*
pepper	**le poivre**	*pwavr*
pork	**le porc**	*por*
potatoes	**les pommes de terre**	*pom-duh tehr*
prawns	**les crevettes**	*kruh-vet*
rice	**le riz**	*ree*
roast	**rôti**	*row-tee*
salt	**le sel**	*sel*
sausage, fresh	**la saucisse**	*sohsees*
seafood	**les fruits de mer**	*frwee duh mer*
shellfish	**les crustacés**	*kroos-ta-say*
soup	**la soupe, le potage**	*soop, poh-tazh*
steak	**le bifteck, le steack**	*beef-tek, stek*
sugar	**le sucre**	*sookr*
tea	**le thé**	*tay*
vegetables	**les légumes**	*lay-goom*
vinegar	**le vinaigre**	*veenaygr*
water	**l'eau**	*l'oh*
red wine	**le vin rouge**	*vañ roozh*
white wine	**le vin blanc**	*vañ bloñ*

Numbers

0	**zéro**	*zeh-roh*
1	**un, une**	*uñ, oon*
2	**deux**	*duh*
3	**trois**	*trwah*
4	**quatre**	*katr*
5	**cinq**	*sañk*
6	**six**	*sees*
7	**sept**	*set*
8	**huit**	*weet*
9	**neuf**	*nerf*
10	**dix**	*dees*
11	**onze**	*oñz*
12	**douze**	*dooz*
13	**treize**	*trehz*
14	**quatorze**	*katorz*
15	**quinze**	*kañz*
16	**seize**	*sehz*
17	**dix-sept**	*dees-set*
18	**dix-huit**	*dees-weet*
19	**dix-neuf**	*dees-nerf*
20	**vingt**	*vañ*
30	**trente**	*tront*
40	**quarante**	*karoñt*
50	**cinquante**	*sañkoñt*
60	**soixante**	*swasoñt*
70	**soixante-dix**	*swasoñt-dees*
80	**quatre-vingts**	*katr-vañ*
90	**quatre-vingt-dix**	*katr-vañ-dees*
100	**cent**	*soñ*
1,000	**mille**	*meel*

Time

one minute	**une minute**	*oon mee-noot*
one hour	**une heure**	*oon urr*
half an hour	**une demi-heure**	*oon duh-me urr*
one day	**un jour**	*un zhorr*
Monday	**lundi**	*luñ-dee*
Tuesday	**mardi**	*mar-dee*
Wednesday	**mercredi**	*mehrkruh-dee*
Thursday	**jeudi**	*zhuh-dee*
Friday	**vendredi**	*voñdruh-dee*
Saturday	**samedi**	*sam-dee*
Sunday	**dimanche**	*dee-moñsh*

Useful Words and Phrases

Yes	**Na**-am
No	Laa
Hello / Peace be upon you	Se**laam**
Goodbye	**Ma**'eel sa**laa**ma
Excuse me	Min **fad**lak
Sorry	Es**me'h**lee
Thank you	**Se**'hha
Please	Min **fad**lak
Good morning	Es**be'h** el**kheer**
Good evening	Ma**saal** kheer
How are you?	Wash**raak?**
I'm fine	**Laa**bas
I don't understand	**A**na mafhim**taksh**
Do you speak English?	Tat**kal**am englee**ze**-ya?
God willing	In**shaal**a
big	k**beer**
small	s**geer**
hot	so**khoon**
cold	**baa**red
bad	mashem**lee**'ha
good	m**lee**'ha
open	maf**too**'h
closed	magh**loo**k
toilet	towa**lett**
a little	ka**leel**
a lot	biz**zaaf**

Emergencies

Stop!	**Ow**kof!
Can you call a doctor?	**Mom**kin **kel**lem el ta**beeb?**
Can you call the police?	**Mom**kin **kel**lem el po**lees**?

Making a Telephone Call

I'd like to speak to…	**Begheet nekallam…**
This is…	**Ha**di…
Please say… called	Min **fad**lak **kol**lo… et**kal**lam

In a Hotel

Do you have a room?	**En**ta '**an**dak **ghor**fa?
With bathroom	Ma'al 'ham-**maam**
single room	**ghor**fa le shakhs **waa**'hid
double room	**ghor**fa le shakh**sayn**
shower	doosh
key	mef**taa**'h

Shopping

How much is it?	Kam el**se'er**?
I'd like…	**A**na 'hab**bayt**
This one	**Ha**di
That's too much	**Ha**di **ghaa**lya
I'll take it	Naa**kho**dha
market	**mar**shee
expensive, cheap	**ghaa**lya, re**khee**sa

Sightseeing

art gallery	gali**ree** daar
beach	b**har**
bus station	stas**yon** do boos
entrance	do**khool**
exit	khrooj
garden	eljo**nay**na
guide	geed
map	kaart
ticket	te**kee**
tourist office	mek**tab** so**yaa**'h
How much is it to…?	Kam te**kal**-laf **haa**zi…?

Eating Out

Have you got a table for…?	**En**ta '**an**dak **tow**la le…?
Can I have the bill please?	Te'e**tee**ni elfa**too**ra min **fad**lak?

Menu Decoder

ta**jee**n	steamed pot of vegetables with meat, etc
kuskus	hand-made couscous
elbas**teel**a	pastry filled with vegetables and meat, etc
'h**ree**ra	soup
kefta	meatballs with herbs
el'**hoo**t	fish
djaaj	chicken
l'hem	meat
le**goom**/**kho**dra	vegetables
maa'a	water

Time

today	el yoom
yesterday	el **baa**reh
tomorrow	**gha**dan
tonight	fel**leel**
day	ne**haar**
hour	**sa'**aa
week	se**maa**na

Days of the Week

Monday	el et**neen**
Tuesday	el t**laa**ta
Wednesday	el ar**be'**aa
Thursday	el kha**mee**s
Friday	el j**o**mo'aa
Saturday	el sa**be**t
Sunday	el a'**had**

Numbers

1	**waa**'hid
2	zooj
3	t**laa**ta
4	ara**ba**'aa
5	**kha**msa
6	**se**t-ta
7	**se**ba'a
8	t**maan**ya
9	**tes**'aa
10	**'a**shra
11	'h**daa**sh
12	et**naa**sh
13	tlat-**taash**
14	erba'-**taash**
15	khmas**taash**
16	set-**taash**
17	sba'a**taash**
18	tman**taash**
19	tas'a**taash**
20	esh**reen**
21	**waa**'hid w'esh**reen**
30	tla**theen**
40	ereb'**een**
50	kham**seen**
60	set-**teen**
70	seb'**een**
80	tma**neen**
90	tes'**een**
100	me**ya**

When you see an apostrophe (') in the Arabic, this means that you pronounce the letter after it with a little puff of air.